STRAITJACKET

Books by Edita Morris

MY DARLING FROM THE LIONS
BIRTH OF AN OLD LADY
THREE WHO LOVED
CHARADE
THE TOIL AND THE DEED
THE SOLO DANCER
LIFE, WONDERFUL LIFE
DEAR ME
THE FLOWERS OF HIROSHIMA
THE SEEDS OF HIROSHIMA
LOVE TO VIETNAM
A HAPPY DAY
HOW KEEPING, HOPE FINE
KILL A BEGGAR
A-FRI-CA
STRAITJACKET

STRAITJACKET

autobiography
EDITA MORRIS

CROWN PUBLISHERS, INC. NEW YORK

Printed in the United States of America

Published simultaneously in Canada
by General Publishing Company Limited
Designed by Ruth Kolbert Smerechniak

Library of Congress Cataloging in Publication Data

Morris, Edita, 1902–
  Straitjacket.

  1. Morris, Edita, 1902– —Biography—
Youth. 2. Novelists, American—20th century—
Biography. 3. Sweden—Biography. I. Title.
PS3525.07376Z47   813'.5'2 [B]   77-28755
ISBN 0-517-53257-3

To Ira

AUTHOR'S NOTE

All persons in this book existed in my life, and every event in the narrative did occur. For my use of the Swedish words in distinguishing family relationships, I ask the reader's indulgence. While these words are too readily identified to be a hindrance to the reader, they were helpful to the author in remembering and writing intimately about her family. For the convenience of the reader, I list the following Swedish words and their English equivalents: mor (mother), far (father), mormor (grandmother), morfar (grandfather), moster (aunt), morbror (mother's brother), farbror (father's brother).

E. M.

STRAITJACKET

"Fuck, it stinks!"

"Cook burned the roast," mormor said. "Don't use that word."

(Word?)

In came Moster Anna, whose tit I'd nibbled in bed. She'd got angry, had locked me out of her room, made me sleep outside her door.

"Something wrong?"

"Edit. At four she swears like a farmhand. She has just used a bad word."

"No wonder. You let her play with the children of workers!"

(Workers? A bad word like fuck?)

"You shan't play with those brats again," snapped Moster Anna.

"Shit-ass!"

A hard hand had never touched me before; I fell over.

"She's fainting!" cried mormor. "Anna, never touch Edit. She's frail! A bird. You don't hit birds, do you?"

Mormor's voice liked me again. I jumped up. I grabbed her hands. "Dance, mormor?"

Oh! We danced! We laughed!

1

"Dance, laugh! That's all Edit is good for," said Moster Anna. "Dance! Laugh!"

———

"What's poor?" I asked cook Frida.

"To have no money."

"Holger says mormor's poor."

"My mormor was poor, too. But she worked. My mormor scrubbed all day! She made sausages all night. She sold her sausages. Ladies don't work. Run off and play. I'm busy."

She flung a ham into the oven.

"Your poor mormor. She has had to buy a new mortgage on Sjögård!"

I ran to the hole that had stuff in it called clay. My legs fell over. They always fell over; my knees always bled. I cried, but no one heard me. I filled my fists with clay. I sat down on my stone, made sausages, got up, ran to a bush, tore off five leaves. I put my clay sausages on the leaves, sat waiting for a buyer.

No one came. It got cold. The sun wasn't where it had been. Where was it? Oh, there it was! A buyer came along. Shit, it was Nilson. He coughed, he always coughed. Someone else came along.

"Want to buy a sausage, mormor?"

"You're still out? You look frozen! It's evening. What are you doing?"

"I'm working. You're poor. I'm selling sausages."

Mormor kneeled beside my flat stone. Her eyes had water in them.

"One sausage costs five öre, mormor."

"I'll buy two, child. Ah, you've arranged them so tastefully on green leaves. You're an artist!"

"Two, mormor?" I gave her two sausages on a leaf.

"Now you've earned ten öre." She gave me ten öre from her pocket.

"Have you sat here all afternoon? To earn money for me? Ah, child, what will you be when you grow up? Who?"

I gave her back ten öre. "Now you're not poor!"

"No, no! Thank you. Thank you."

"Well, take them, mormor. Buy yourself a mortgage. The money's yours."

"That's who you'll become when you grow up," cried mormor. "A . . . giver!"

"The horde's arriving," Moster Anna said.

"Horde?"

"Lots of awful family!"

An extra table had been moved into the dining room. At the big table sat mor, mormor, Moster Anna, Morbror Vilhelm, five more aunts, five more uncles, and neighbor Ryberg. At the children's table sat my eleven cousins, my three sisters, myself. "We're twenty-nine," I said.

"You know how to count? Edit knows how to count," my eldest sister Greta told my cousins.

"That anchovy," they sneered.

"Schs-ss!" said a voice from the big table.

"Do you know how to read, too?" asked Greta.

I didn't know my sisters. They were bigger, older.

3

I only saw them during the holidays. They never bothered about me.

"Do you know how to read, too?" Greta asked again. I nodded. "She knows how to read!" she told my cousins. "At four! Who taught you?"

I pointed to myself.

"What's that thing that has two stomachs poking out?" I'd asked cook.

"It's a *B*," Frida said.

"What's that one?"

"An *A*. *B* and *A* make *Ba*. Like a sheep."

"What's that silly ass?"

"It's a *G*. *B*—*A*—*G* makes *Bag*."

"*Bag?*" I laughed. All that day I said *ba* inside of me: *ba, ba, bag, bag*. All that winter I said *tool, fool, muck, fuck*. I learned all the letters, I loved all the letters; I loved the words the letters made. When the birch tree got green in May, I sat down under it, and read a newspaper.

Now at the big table, neighbor Ryberg was telling mormor: "Sjögård isn't run properly. You are losing money. I hear you've taken out a new mortgage. Soon you'll be forced to sell Sjögård."

"Sell? Sjögård!"

"In the end, yes. Let me give you a piece of advice," neighbor Ryberg said. "Work your farmhands harder!"

"They do work hard, Hanns!"

"Ten hours a day isn't work. It's play. When I ran the sugar beet plant, we hired Poles for the harvests. Those animals slaved fourteen hours a day. Of course I carried a whip," he laughed.

"A whip!" exclaimed my five aunts.

"What for?" their five husbands said.

"Well, not to caress the Poles with," laughed neighbor Ryberg.

"I'm baking. Get out of my kitchen," Frida told Maud.

"Your kitchen?" snapped my sister. "Everything in Sjögård belongs to mormor."

"Till neighbor Ryberg moves in," said Frida. "He's courting your Aunt Anna so's to get Sjögård. It's Sjögård he wants! Not your long-nosed moster."

Frida shoved a pan with buns into the oven. "The day neighbor Ryberg moves in, I move out. That slave driver! We'll all leave Sjögård!" Frida shouted.

"Neighbor Ryberg can get you blacklisted," said Maud. "He'll stop you from getting jobs!"

"He can't stop us from emigrating. Emigration agents come along the first of every month. We'll all sail to a new nation. To USA!"

"Nation!" Maud said. "Sweden is a nation. France, Germany, are nations. America is a trash can full of immigrants. They don't even have a language of their own. They jabber something they think is English. America's all right for trash. Trash like you, Frida!"

Frida threw a dish cloth at her.

"Get out!"

"You stay," she told me. "Here's a bun, fresh from the oven, hot as a mouse."

I squeezed the ant's waist.

"Child! What are you doing?"

"I'm squeezing the ant's waist. Where have you come from?" I asked.

5

"Stockholm," mor said, "Have you forgotten me? Oh, child, don't pinch the ant's waist. Let it go. Have pity on the poor ant."

(Pity?)

Mor sat down on the grass. She smelled of roses. I sniffed at her. Shit! The fart-ant wanted to get away from me. I squeezed it harder.

"You'll sever its waist," said mor.

I shrieked with laughter, and pinched harder.

"Ah, child, become the ant. Then you'll know how the ant's waist aches when you squeeze it. You'll feel in your own body how the poor ant wants to get away. Be the ant, Edit!"

"A-ou!"

"You see?" mor said. "You cried out with pain. Why? Because you'd become the ant. Your body ached because it had become the ant's body. Pity is to become . . . someone else. Never forget it."

"Forget what, mor?"

"A little girl," sighed mor. "A little girl's frightening. A little girl understands nothing. Yet, who knows? Perhaps you'll understand pity one day. Pity."

"The shit-ant's run off," I said.

———

"Want to see Hercules screw?" asked Holger. "His stick is as long as my arm."

"His stick?"

We climbed to the hay loft. "Edit's going to watch Hercules screw. Move over," Holger told our playmates. His tongue shoved his wad of snuff to the other cheek. Mormor said Holger was too young to

6

chew snuff, too young to drink schnaps. Holger said
he did a man's work, so he'd drink like a man. "Anyhow, I'm eleven."

"Here he comes!" Holger said.

Nilson led out the bull. Olle led out the cow.

"Look at Hercules' stick!" said Holger.

"Where is it?"

"Under his stomach, idiot. Mine will be like that
when I'm a man."

Hercules' stick was long, I wondered how it'd fit
inside Holger's trousers. The bull bellowed. I was
scared. I closed my eyes. When I opened them the bull
had his front legs on the cow's back.

"He has lost his stick!"

"It's inside the cow, stupid ass," Holger said. A
louse crawled from his hair to his lip. He swallowed
it. "I eat lice instead of meat. A louse costs nothing."

"Look," he said, "Hercules is coming!"

"Where?"

"Inside the cow, stupid shit-brat. The cow'll have
a calf. You'll have a brat, too, after you've been
poked."

"Poked?"

"Hercules is poking, for crissake. Don't you see
his ass grinding? It makes his stuff shoot into the cow.
That's how your mormor got five girls, one boy."

"Hercules poked mormor?"

"No your morfar poked her."

"Alfhild, Bärta, want to play bull?" Holger asked
our playmates.

"Can I play?"

"Run away, shit-brat."

Alfhild, Bärta lay down in the hay. They pulled
up their rags. They had no pants.

"Come on, Holger," said Alfhild. "Fart-brat," she

told me, "if you tell your mormor we'll knock your teeth out of your fucking head!"

"Tell mormor what?"

"About your morfar's stick. Come on, Holger!"

———

"Why are you trundling earwigs about in a cart?" laughed Morbror Vilhelm. "And what are those other horrors?"

"Wood lice. I'm taking them for a ride."

"A ride!"

"I pick them out from under the bark. They enjoy riding."

"How do you know?" asked Morbror Vilhelm.

"Mor said I should become an ant."

"An ant? And now you've become a wood louse? Well, I must be off! Have a nice ride, earwigs. Have a lovely afternoon, horrors."

I set off too. The earwigs twirled their pincers. Oh! They liked their ride!

———

The hens were feeding. The cock shoved them away, ate their swill.

"That'll teach you." I hurled a stone at his face that had swill on it.

"You've killed the rooster!" cried Moster Anna.

"Killed him?"

"My beautiful cock! He'll never love his hens

8

again. Never greet another sunrise. He's dead!"

"Dead?"

"To be dead is to be not alive. It's the most terrible thing on earth. We'll all die. You! me! Yes, I, too, will lie still one day."

That made me laugh. "Why doesn't the rooster get up?" I asked.

"I've told you. He's dead."

"Can't one get up when one's dead?" I laughed.

"All you do is to laugh. Laugh, laugh. Oh, my rooster!"

"I'm taking my passengers back to their holes," I said. "Come on, wood lice."

———

"Alfhild, Bärta, what ails your mother?" asked mormor.

"We don't know."

"But I no longer see her about. Is she up?"

"No."

"Does she eat?"

"No."

"Speak?"

"No."

"Cough?"

"Yes!"

"Alfhild and Bärta are leftovers from another age," mormor told us before the fireplace. "Farmhands accept life like dumb beasts. Their children too."

"Who made them into dumb beasts?" said Morbror Vilhelm. "Think back. In the seventeenth century, we cut off a peasant's hand if we caught him

9

stealing. In the eighteenth, we chased him from his farm if he couldn't pay murderous taxes. When he dragged himself off to the towns to beg, we robbed him of his begging permit."

"You make Sweden sound barbarous," sighed mormor. "Our history has brighter sides. Remember Sweden's Great-Power Days! Gustavus Adolphus . . ."

"Sweden starved to death, while that mass murderer fought in the Thirty Years War. Way, way off in Germany! For his own glory!"

"What about his daughter, Kristina? Kristina adorned her court with scholars of great erudition."

"Which didn't stop her from having peasant women flogged when they filched tufts of hay to feed their starving offspring. During the reign of your erudite Kristina, children were found dead in the snow with tufts of hay in their mouths.

"Sweden is still a barbarous country," Morbror Vilhelm went on. "That's why entire villages emigrate, mor. There are more Swedes in America today than in Sweden. The shame of it. Only crippled oldsters and consumptives stay in Sweden."

"Consumptives, Morbror Vilhelm?" I asked.

"People who cough, child."

Mormor held up her hand. "Don't explain about consumption to Edit. She remembers everything. She has nightmares about everything she hears. Child, run out and play."

I ran out. Alfhild and Bärta passed me in the dark. They coughed. Consumptives? I didn't call out to them. I grabbed a tuft of hay from the dog's house, lay down in the snow. I stuffed my mouth full of hay.

———

"We've finished," Morbror Vilhelm said. We were standing near the station in Sölvesborg. He looked up from the shopping list mormor had given him. "We'll fetch Moster Anna. She went to the station to pick up a package with a dress."

Something with red eyes dashed by us.

"Where's that thing dashing to?" I asked Morbror Vilhelm.

"The train? It'll stop here a few minutes. To pick up the emigrants. That lot over there carrying cooking utensils. Carrying mattresses."

A hag with a coffeepot in one hand, a night pot in the other, didn't want to get on the train. An emigrant pushed her in. She screamed. The emigrants all climbed onto the train.

"They're weeping," I said.

"You'd weep too if you had to leave your country. Poor creatures! They're going to America to sell their hands."

(Hands?)

Moster Anna came hopping along. "Where's her package?" I said. "Shit! She looks angry."

"How hideous they are," said Moster Anna. "One never notices how starved our farmhands look. Vilhelm, I can't get the package with my dress till the train has left. Don't they look hideous?"

I looked at the emigrants. They looked like Karlson. They looked like Nilson. They looked like Sven, like Olle.

"Will they have their hands cut off in the station, Morbror Vilhelm?"

"Cut off? Their hands! Child, selling one's hands doesn't mean they're cut off," Morbror Vilhelm said. "Stop trembling." He sighed. "Ah, the poor wretches will be treated like dirt in America."

11

"They're treated like dirt right here," Moster Anna said. "We Swedes are as ferocious exploiters as the Americans. You, too. You're an exploiter for all your sweet ways, Vilhelm!"

The hag with the night pot jumped off the train that had begun to move. She fell. She broke her bones. Crack! An emigrant hauled her back on the train.

"Let's get out of here!" cried Moster Anna. "Now I can get my package. The dress I ordered is sweet. Pink."

The train ran off. The night pot was left on the platform.

———

It was night. I screamed, "Moster Anna!"

She didn't answer. At the foot of my bed was the garret, I heard people dragging about in there. In a minute they'd reach my bed.

"They're coming for me, Moster Anna!" I howled. "Moster Anna! They have no hands!"

"It's only mice playing in the garret. Let me sleep," cried Moster Anna from her safe room.

I jumped out of my bed and ran to her door.

I banged it. I kicked it.

"Let me in!"

I heard Moster Anna breathe in her bed. The steps from the garret came closer. I didn't dare turn my head. I knew the people without hands would put their stumps on the back of my neck. I heard blood drip from their stumps.

"Let me in," I screamed. "Let me in!"

"Go back to your bed," Moster Anna said. "Go back to sleep!"

"Help!" I howled. Something happened to my body that sometimes happened to my body. It fell over. It lay on the floor with me inside it.

"You let Edit faint outside your door, Anna?" cried mormor. "Edit is frail. You may have ruined her nervous system for good."

"How could I know she'd faint from fright?" yawned Moster Anna.

Morbror Vilhelm carried me away. "You'll sleep in mormor's room from now on. In morfar's empty bed. You'll feel safe, Edit."

(Never safe again, never safe again!)

"Don't tremble," Morbror Vilhelm said. "Oh, I've just remembered such a funny story," he laughed. He put me down in morfar's bed.

"It's about a centipede. Two rabbits lived in a room beneath a centipede. Every night they heard 'Boum! Boum!' from the centipede's room. 'Go up and see what the centipede's up to,' the rabbit's wife told her husband. He ran upstairs. Oh, what was happening? Well, Edit, it was the centipede taking off his hundred shoes before getting into bed! One by one, he hurled them on the floor. Boum! Boum!"

"The people came for me from the garret, Morbror Vilhelm. They had no hands!"

"We'll send for the doctor in the morning," whispered mormor. "Edit's delirious. I don't know what she means by no hands?"

"*I* know!" Morbror Vilhelm said.

———

I began to be frightened of everything in dark Sjö-gård. I began to hate dark Sjögård. I stopped eating. I stopped sleeping. I refused to go out of doors. I was afraid my nose would freeze and fall into the snow.

"Go out and play," ordered Moster Anna. "You're as pale as a potato, you're as thin as a sewing needle. You need air!"

I went out, but I didn't stay out. I never stayed out. I started to run toward our coachman's cottage.

"If I catch you playing in the farmhands' cottages, I'll whip you black and blue," Moster Anna shouted after me. "Their shacks crawl with lice! Their hovels are alive with germs. Everyone coughs their lungs out. Ten people live in one room."

I arrived at Nilson's shack. I counted on my fingers: Alfhild, Bärta, two; mormor-morfar, four; Nilson, five; his brother, six; the new twins, eight; a witch lived with them, nine; Holger lived with them, ten.

"We're cleaning under morfar-mormor," Alfhild said. "We're putting clean straw under them. Bring a pail of water, Holger."

Mormor-morfar lived in bed. They'd been broken by work in Sjögård, Holger had told me. He said they couldn't stand on their legs. If they wanted to sit up in bed, they heaved themselves forward by a rope that dangled before their faces.

"Give us a potato, son," morfar-mormor begged Nilson. They doubled up, coughing.

"Stop coughing!" shouted Nilson to his parents, and began to cough himself. His wife had coughed the most. She had died three days ago.

"Holger, let's play over at Karlson's," I said.

He grabbed my hand. "Show you something funny," he said. But he didn't take me to Karlson's shack; he took me to the river behind it. "Look!" He laughed. *"Look!"*

Karlson and his wife half stood on the bottom of

the frozen river. Karlson was holding onto his bottle of schnaps. His wife held onto Karlson.

"He got drunk," Holger said. "Karna dragged him home. He hit her. They fought. They fell into the river. The river froze over last night. They'll stand there till the spring thaw."

"Ho-ho-ho," laughed Holger.

———

We went back to Nilson's, we stepped into his hen house. A hen turned her tail to us; an egg sat in the white feathers of the hen's tail; the egg fell into Holger's hand. It was nice; it looked warm.

But outside the snow pelted down. The wind smacked the hen house. I hated the snow. I hated the wind, the dark. I hated dark Sjögàrd.

"I'm going to Stockholm," I told Holger.

"Who says so?"

"I!"

"I'll give you my egg if you don't go."

"Your egg? For keeps?"

"If you don't go!"

"I won't go if you give me your egg."

Holger gave me his egg. It was still warm.

"I won't go!" I said.

———

I fell ill.

"That Edit!" said Moster Anna. "That pin!"

I stayed in bed. At night Bengta came to read to

me. She took off her clogs, dropped me a curtsy, sat on the edge of morfar's big bed, read aloud from *Allers Weekly Journal*.

I didn't understand what Bengta read. I didn't listen. Under my blanket, I squeezed Holger's egg. "I won't go to Stockholm," I promised it.

Bengta read on. She smelled of safe cow, but I no longer felt safe in dark Sjögård. Every night people came for me with stumps where their hands had been. Every morning I had fever.

"I'm going," I told Holger's egg. "I'm going to Stockholm!"

Holger's egg didn't like what I told it.

"I won't go," I promised. "I'll stay."

———

Bengta read on. I fell asleep. A sleigh drawn by horses with bells round their necks stopped outside the house. Someone flew up the stairs, flew into my room, took me in her arms. They smelled of roses.

"I'm taking you back with me to Stockholm. At once!" whispered mor. "Mormor wrote that you are losing weight. The doctor said you're losing weight fast. Get up, child."

Oh! We ran off, we drove off. The horses' bells said: "Ping."

I woke up. "I'm going to Stockholm, Bengta," I told our milkwoman.

She didn't answer. Bengta never answered.

She only spoke to cows. She got up, dropped a curtsy, went out. I longed, longed for mor who smelled of roses.

16

"Mormor, come here," I shouted. "Quick! Come, mormor!"

Mormor came.

"I want to go to mor," I wept. "I want to go to mor in Stockholm. To mor!"

———

It happened as I'd dreamed. Mormor had written that I'd become thinner than a sewing needle. Mor came to fetch me. We jumped into the sleigh, the horses' bells said: "Ping." Nilson whipped his horses. Snow pelted down on us.

"We'll turn into snowmen," said mor. Her little nose smiled at me.

We got to the station, waited for the train: "We'll turn into icicles," said mor. Her little nose smiled at me.

"The train!"

"We're traveling third class. We're poor. I'm just divorced."

"Divorced?"

"Well, far and I don't live together. I've left him. I never liked far."

"Shit."

"It's time I took you away from the country." Mor smiled. "Your language! In Stockholm, you'll play with nice children."

(Alfhild-Bärta-Holger weren't *nice?* I hadn't known.)

"The duck is peeing on me."

"Your language, Edit!"

"It's peeing lots!"

17

A peasant's trussed-up duck sat above my head in the rack beside my suitcase.

"Go to the lavatory, Edit. Wash yourself," mor said. "It's at the end of the corridor."

I washed myself. There was no towel. I felt in my coat pockets for something to dry my hands on. My fingers touched Holger's egg. Holger's egg! I'd forgotten his egg. The train gave a lurch. Was I on a train? The train was taking me away from Holger! Away . . . from . . . Holger. I fell over.

"What are you doing in here so long?" asked mor. "Why are you on the floor? You're white! What's the matter, child? Come back to our compartment, quick!"

I was wearing my snowcap. One could lower the flaps so that one's face didn't show. I lowered the flaps. But my eyes showed.

"You're crying! Have you got such a great sorrow?" mor whispered to me.

(Sorrow?)

Water ran from her eyes as she looked at me. I laughed. I had never seen a big person cry before. Oh! I laughed. Then I remembered that Holger wouldn't be in Stockholm when we got there.

"Mor, I want to go back to Sjögård! Tell the train to turn round," I said.

"I can't. One can't ask them to turn the train and go back. Our train's going full speed! We'll be in Stockholm in the evening."

But Holger wouldn't be in Stockholm in the evening. I hadn't known that Holger and I could be in two different places! I took a step toward the window. I yanked it down. I tried to throw myself out. I'd run back to Sjögård! I'd run back to Holger!

"What are you doing, Edit? You are trying to fall

out? Oh, child," whispered mor, "have you got such a very big sorrow?"

Mor opened her arms. I jumped into her arms that smelled of roses. Of roses.

———

"She dances, mor!"

"Who?"

"Stockholm!"

"Those are the gas lights." Mor's voice didn't sound like other voices, it sounded like a bee's. "Of course, you've never been to a city before, child. Well, Edit, we have arrived."

Mor talked on. I never listened when people talked on. Outside the train, the lights of Stockholm danced. I wanted to dance.

"We're just coming into the Central Station. Here! Take your little suitcase, child," mor said. She jumped into Stockholm. I jumped into Stockholm.

We got into a horse cab.

"I don't take cabs any more," said mor. Her voice wasn't louder than a bee's. "I've no money. But one can't get on a tram with luggage. Sit down, child!"

I stood up. I'd never sit down in lit-up Stockholm. I'd stand up!

I began to sing.

"You don't have much of a voice, do you? Your pitch is all wrong."

I sang louder. I sang, I laughed. I danced in the cab.

"You're such a . . . gay little girl." Mor smiled.

"So . . . funny! It'll be nice to have you about in our little flat. Your sisters are so big—and self-centered. They don't care for me any more."

On the streets of Stockholm, everyone ran. Except some bundles that lay in the doorways.

"What are the bundles?" I asked.

"Don't look, Edit. They aren't bundles. They are poor people who have nowhere to sleep except in doorways."

"They can sleep in my bed."

"Child. They're drunks. Down-and-outers. Soon they'll be dead. They're beggars."

"Beggars?"

"People who can't find work beg. There are thousands of them. There are tens of thousands of them in Sweden. No one gives them work. Then they steal. Then the police take them. Then they're thrown in jail. Then they come out of jail, starve, die."

Police? Jail? Beggars? I hadn't heard those words in Sjögård. I must learn the new Stockholm words. *Police. Jail. Beggars.*

"Mor, I don't want to stay in Stockholm. I don't like the bundles."

———

Two beauties stood in the open door when mor and I arrived from the station.

"You haven't seen your big sisters for a year. A whole year!" said mor. She put down my suitcase.

(Sisters? Those beauties were my *sisters?*)

They kissed me. A great plain one came in, too; she too kissed me. Her, I recognized. It was my sister

20

Greta. She was eight years older than myself. Then some lump arrived.

"This is Hanna. She was farmor's maid," mor said. "When farmor died, Hanna came to us," mor said.

Hanna didn't curtsy to me like Bengta in Sjö-gård. She had on a dress with white dots, an apron with white frills. I wanted to lick her terribly clean face.

The two beauties smiled at me. "Mor, you must make Edit a new outfit. A Stockholm outfit. We'll show her off to our friends."

I threw myself into their arms.

"The child must go to bed. Edit's had a long day in the train," plain Greta said.

"Must is your favorite word, Greta," laughed the beauties. "You always want people to do what they don't want to do." They laughed again. I laughed. I clung to the beauties.

"You've the longest hair I've ever seen," Elsa said.

"I can sit on my hair."

"Show us!"

I sat on my hair.

The beauties laughed. "Oh, mor, she's charming!" they said. "Gay. She has dimples like holes."

"Off to bed!" Plain Greta grabbed my arm. I tore myself away.

"What else can you do except sitting on your hair?"

"Read. Write. Carry dung."

"Now I am putting her to bed," cried Greta. She led me away. I kicked her shin.

"Fuck-ass! Stink-fart!"

"Edit!" cried mor.

"Mor, she's so funny," laughed the beauties, "so funny! A charmbag!"

(Charmbag?)

Plain Greta lifted her hand to smack me. Mor hurried over to her. "Never touch Edit!" she said. "Edit is a . . . she's a . . . a . . ."

"Yes," cried the beauties, "She is, she is."

———

Mor's needle ran in, ran out.

"Are you making me a dress?" I asked her.

"And a coat. An outfit for Stockholm. I make all our clothes. We're so very poor."

I put on my Stockholm outfit. The coat was of brown velveteen. The bonnet was of brown velveteen; it tied under my chin. The beauties grabbed my hands, flew down the streets with me; on the street they ran into friends.

"This is our small sister, Edit," they laughed.

The friends laughed, too. I laughed. They smiled at me. I flung myself in their arms.

"Oh, but she's simply charming. Is she always so . . . gay?" they asked.

The friends took my hands.

"I want to walk her," one of them said.

"No, I," laughed the other.

"We'll take her in turns," they said.

"Shit-brat!" a boy shouted to me. "Have you exchanged legs with a rooster?" He pointed to my thin legs. He stood on the street corner with lots of boys, picking his nose.

"Rooster-legs!" they shouted at me. Their toes

stuck out from their boots. Their noses ran. They had
long yellow hair like Holger. They stuck out their
tongues at me like Holger. Oh! I wanted to stay and
play with them. I stuck out my tongue at them, as far
as it would go.

"Edit! Come away. They're dangerous," hissed
my sisters. "They're the street boys of Stockholm.
They steal! They knife people. Come."

I shook my head. I liked the street boys. They
looked like my playmates in Sjögård. But my beautiful
sisters hated them: so I must hate them, too. If I could
find a stone, I'd make a snowball with a rock inside
it. I'd hurl it at the street boys. I picked up a handful
of snow. I threw it at the street boys.

"Shit-brat!" they howled.

"Shit-brats yourselves! Fuck-asses!"

"Edit!" my sisters said. They didn't like me any
more. I didn't like them. I liked the street boys. They
spat after me, I spat at them. They howled. They
swore. They began to chase us. My sisters grabbed my
hands. We fled.

"You're a savage," my sisters said. "Ugh!"

"She's a savage," the beauties told each other.
"She's stayed too long in Sjögård. Too long in the awful countryside."

(Savage?)

In number four, Stureparken, I grew myself dizzy,
it took all of my time to grow. I also wrote stories, and
drew pictures for them. Sang.

"Schs-ss!" said my sisters.

My sisters didn't like me any more. I didn't care.

23

I'd fallen in love. I'd fallen in love with someone who sat playing all day at her piano, who sat huddled all evening before her fire. With a woman whose eyes always wept.

"Let's laugh, mor."

"You laugh."

I laughed. She laughed, too. I threw myself into her arms that smelled of roses. "I love you!"

"I love you," she said. "I love you."

"Then why do you weep?"

"I'm lonesome. I am no longer married. I didn't like your father. But I can't bear my lonesomeness!"

"I'll marry you."

I made two small bows, sewed a blue bead on each of them. I fastened them to two safety pins, pinned one on mor, one on myself. "Now we're married."

I laughed, but mor wept.

She got up and sat down at her piano, but her hands lay in her lap. They looked like small white gloves.

"Play, mor."

She played. "It's a love song. By Grieg." She told me about Grieg, wept again.

"Now why do you weep, mor?"

"Someone who once loved me . . . went away. He wasn't far. He was someone else. I've given up."

"What is it, to give up?"

Mor's nose smiled. It was small. It was white. I wanted to lick it.

"Two frogs fell into a bowl of milk," said mor. "One of them cried, 'I'm drowning!' He threw his arms in the air . . . drowned. The other frog churned round the bowl of milk all night. In the morning he sat on a pat of butter. I . . . I drowned, child."

"I'll sit on a pat of butter!"

"Child."

"You'll sit beside me! Everyone will sit beside me!"

———

In the evenings my big sisters stuck their fingers in their ears, their noses in their grammars. I brought my story books to the kitchen, settled myself in the sofa that was Hanna. Her lap was big. I thought of Hanna as my sofa. I was astonished when I heard it breathe. I read, drew pictures. When my sofa began to snore, I craned my neck to stare into the hole from where the snores came. Had Hanna sat snoring in the kitchen for ever? A hundred years?

"Have you sat here for a hundred years, Hanna?" Hanna woke up.

"I've worked for the countess all my life, child."

"The countess?"

"Your farmor, for heaven's sake! She was born a Countess Horn. She married your father's father. He was General Toll. He died. I stayed on with the countess. She died. Your mother inherited the antiques that came from the countess' home, the manor of Åminne. They were loaded on a horse van. I sat on top."

"On top of what?"

"On top of the countess's writing desk. The little one in the drawing room."

"Why don't you ever sit in the drawing room, Hanna?" I asked. "Must you stay in the kitchen?"

"The drawing room? Child, you don't know what you're saying! Goodness!" cried Hanna. "Heavens!" Hanna cried. "I hope I know my place."

(My place?)

25

"You're no longer a child," my sister Elsa told me in the park.

"I'm eight. Yesterday I was eight."

"You had a nice birthday. Now you're big. Well, that's my point. One becomes a new person every seventh year. You must no longer think like a child, you must no longer act like a child. Do you understand?"

I shook my head.

"It's comfortable to remain a child," Elsa said, "but one mustn't! Look at the little boy pedaling on his tricycle over there. He'll do it all morning— round, round. He isn't ridiculous! Because he's only three. If he tricycled around all morning when he was ten, he'd be ridiculous. If he tricycled round and round when he was twenty, he'd be put in a lunatic asylum."

She sat thinking on our bench in Stureparken.

"It's all right to do certain things for a certain length of time," Elsa said. "Overnight it becomes absurd! Tomorrow you'll start school, Edit. Being you, it will be difficult."

School was easy.

I sat down in a room with desks. "You're Edit Toll," a dwarf said. She read from a letter. "Your health is frail. That's why you had to live in the country. That's why you are a year late starting school. I must find out what you know. Can you read?"

I nodded.

"Then read this!"

I read a silly story. The dwarf's mouth opened. "I'm . . . amazed. You read with the speed, the accuracy of an adult. Did you like the story?"

"Shit, no!"

"Dear *girl!* Well, what's wrong with the story? And may one ask how you know?"

"I write."

"Well, seeing your skill in reading and writing, you may skip a class. You'll move straight up into the second preparatory class." Dwarf got up. She wasn't much taller than me.

"Why are you so small?" I asked her.

"I wish I knew." She had water in her eyes. "It's my tragedy! All of us have tragedies. Laugh when yours come along."

"Are you a teacher?" I asked. "Is this a school?"

"It is the best girls' school in the world, Edit. Always remember that. Sweden, educationally speaking, surpasses all countries. In Sweden, culture means more than money and power." Dwarf put her small hand on my shoulder. "I shall enjoy teaching you, Edit. I shall enjoy you."

A stick with spectacles stomped in.

"A new pupil, Edit Toll, a relative to General Karl Toll. An . . . an unusual little girl!" said dwarf. Stick stomped away. I put my tongue out after her. Dwarf did the same.

"Does that look attractive—my putting out my tongue?" she asked me. "Don't you think that tongues are less ugly inside one's face—on the whole?"

(On the whole?)

"Keep your tongue inside your face, Edit. You come from a well-bred family. Behave like a member of a well-bred family." Dwarf laughed. "What one does inside one is no one's business!"

———

I made my vocabulary grow like a mushroom because of my new dictionary with a globe on its cover. I loved every word. I understood few of them!

Three short words haunted my childhood: *poor, noble, fear.*

We were very "poor." But that was the least important.

I belonged to the ancient Swedish "nobility." The fact that I was "the Honorable Edit Toll" set me apart from girls named Karlson, Nilson, Svenson. We were three "nobles" in my class: Agnes, Elsa, Edit. We were set apart from the other girls. My sister Elsa said: "We stay apart the way racehorses in a paddock stay apart from dray horses."

Between classes, the little girls linked hands with their best friends and hopped, in pairs, up and down the corridors. Outside it was always black; snow poured down. In the corridors, we got our exercise.

I hopped with Agnes Weidenhielm. Her father was a high officer. Agnes was my best friend.

"Will you hop with me?" asked Elsa Rosenblad.

I hopped with her. She became my friend, too. Her father was equerry to the king.

I hopped with no one else.

At home, one day, I made a discovery. "Hanna, you're to stand up when I speak to you," my sister Maud told Hanna. "I'm a noble. You're a commoner! I am the Honorable Maud Toll!"

But Hanna didn't get up. "You're a noble because your father is a nobleman," she said. "I'm a commoner because my father was gardener at General Toll's. If your father had been a gardener and mine a nobleman, you'd be a commoner."

"You're impudent! I'll tell mor on you."

"She's a commoner, too."

"*Mor?*"

Maud's hand was raised to slap Hanna, but mor's hand stopped her. "Never strike a servant! Never speak roughly to someone who can't answer back. Do you hear me, Maud?"

"Grandfather struck his orderlies," Maud said. Her eyes looked like blue pebbles.

"Your paternal grandfather was known as a brute," said mor. "He belonged to medieval times. There still isn't a law in Sweden forbidding masters to lay hand on their servants, but nobody hits their servants any more. Your grandfather made a deal with his orderly. Every time he struck him, he, the General, would pay his orderly twenty-five öre. A shameful arrangement."

Mor put her hand over her eyes. It looked like a little white glove. When she took it away, her nose had got white. "Your Grandfather Toll was hated by his sons! He ruined your father's character."

"Hanna told a lie, mor," Maud said. "That's why I wanted to slap her. She said you are a commoner!"

"I am."

"*Mor!*"

"Naturally. I have my father's name. It's a very ordinary name."

———

That night in our bedroom, Maud stamped her foot. "Imagine. Our mother a commoner! It must be dreadful not to be a noble."

"Is that why she weeps?" Maud asked Elsa. "Because she wasn't born a Toll?"

"I don't choose to answer you," Elsa said. "You were rude to Hanna. You were rude to a human being. Hanna is a human being."

"Hanna a human being? Hanna is a domestic."

Greta was asleep; I was in my bed; Maud jumped into hers. Elsa began to brush her hair in the light of the petrol lamp.

"We're used to servants being treated like dogs in Sweden," she said. "You, Maud, really didn't know that Hanna was a human being? Hanna's been worked to the bone since she was fourteen. She has been paid next to nothing like all servants in our country. Domestics in Sweden are given slops to eat—skim milk and potatoes."

"Oh, shut up!" Maud said. "Put out the light. I want to get my beauty sleep. I want to look my best for my party tomorrow!"

Elsa lifted her hairbrush. She hit Maud hard.

"Does Hanna get any beauty sleep? Does she even have a room to sleep in?" she said, threatening to hit Maud again. "Hanna sleeps in a hole! Almost all servants' rooms in Stockholm are unheated holes behind the kitchens. We store lots of junk in those holes— broken chairs, unwanted clothes. Why? Because a servant's room isn't hers. Servant maids aren't even allowed to lock their doors."

"They'd have men in their beds if they were given keys," giggled Maud. "Servant maids are bitches."

Elsa whacked her again with her hairbrush.

Maud howled as Elsa hit her again and again. I'd never seen Elsa like that before. Were there two Elsas?

"Servants are human beings!" she cried with each blow.

"No, bitches," shouted Maud.

"They're human beings!" Elsa repeated.

But Maud had dropped off to sleep. She looked like an angel. She snored softly like an angel snores.

———

Of the three words that haunted my childhood, *fear* was the worst.

"Tomorrow is the first of May. You're not to go out of doors, girls," mor said. Her voice shook with fright.

"Not go out? Why?"

"The first of May is the workers' day. You don't know workers. I do. I lived through the General Strike of nineteen nine. It scared me for life. It maimed our whole class."

"Mor!" said Elsa.

"I know what I am talking about. Tomorrow, the first of May, Stockholm's workers will march to Lily-ans Woods to listen to their leader. To that agitator, Branting!"

Her little nose was white again. I wanted to caress it. I wanted to take mor on my lap.

"The workers will parade through the streets of Stockholm, waving their red flags."

"Red, mor?"

"Red is the color of . . . of . . ."

"Hanna's niece says it's the color of International

Labor. Whatever that is." Maud laughed, but mor wrung her hands.

"The government may call out the military. In nineteen nine members of our family shot at the striking workers." Mor trembled. "Ah, I hate shooting. Shooting isn't . . . nice. But workers are bandits! Tomorrow they might break into our flat and steal your Grandmother Horn's antiques."

I dived into mor's sofa before the fire. I put a cushion over my head. I was shaking with fear.

"Mor! Lock the front door. Lock it, mor!"

"It is locked, Edit. Bolted."

But *fear* had entered into my mind for good.

———

I ran to the kitchen to get an apple. Hanna's niece sat on the apple crate. "Would you get up?" I asked her, but Gärda didn't move. She was talking to Hanna, who slept by the stove.

"I thought I'd look in on you on my way from the meeting, Moster Hanna. In Lilyans Woods. Oh! It was a big demonstration. Everyone cried, 'Down with the military!' 'Death to the blood suckers!' "

"Gärda, you oughtn't to be here," Hanna said. Sometimes she was hard of hearing but her niece's shouting woke her up. "Hurry back to your work in the hotel."

"I've joined the Social Democrats, Moster Hanna!" shouted Gärda. "Many of us have. The chambermaids in Grand Hotel. The hotel exploits us, Moster Hanna. We're demanding an eight-hour working day."

"Go and play," Hanna told me.

The tip of Gärda's chin stuck out like a nose. It looked wild. In her excitement she jumped off the apple crate, and I grabbed an apple before she threw herself down on the crate again. "Moster Hanna, the military are the paid servants of Capital! Did you know that?"

"Edit, go and play," Hanna said again.

"Who was shouting in the kitchen?" mor asked, "Crazy Gärda?"

I nodded. I laughed. "Down with the military," I shouted. "Down with the military!"

"That was the workers' slogan in the nineteen nine strike!" Mor began to weep. "Your sisters say I am stupid. Stupid to have let nineteen nine scare me. It scared Tant Hedvig! Tant Maja! Everyone of us. Terrible workers from America, Germany, France, sent money to the Swedish strikers. They'll do so again! They call it solidarity. Or something like that!"

"Will they cut off our heads, mor?" I asked.

We were doing homework beneath the petrol lamp. It smoked. I chewed my pencil. My two eldest sisters were at the top of their class, I was at the bottom of mine.

"You never do any homework," Greta scolded. She always scolded everyone. "What are you sitting staring at, Edit?"

"At a ham."

"A—ham!" laughed Maud.

I laughed too. But I didn't answer. I never spoke

33

about the pictures that hung on the walls of my inside-head. But I often looked at them. Just now I was looking at a ham, remembering that day in Sjögård when I'd accompanied mormor on her monthly inspection tour of the cupboards and the larders. She'd showed the cook cluttered shelves and dangling cobwebs, ordered her to sweep out corners and to scrub the walls.

In a back larder, she'd called, "Frida! What's that ham doing on the top shelf? Right at the back?" She pointed at something big and brown.

"Minding its own business," laughed Morbror Vilhelm, who had tagged along. "Someone put the ham there. Someone forgot to take it away. Simple!"

"Get it down for me, Vilhelm," mormor said. "You're tall."

"But I'm not a giraffe," smiled Morbror Vilhelm. "Please bring me a broom, Frida."

My mouth watered. The ham looked good. Vilhelm poked at it with Frida's broom.

"It's coming down," he said.

Oh! The ham toppled over. It hit the stone floor. It burst open.

"Maggots!" Mormor screamed.

Maggots slithered out of the rotten ham by the thousands. I wanted to vomit; I forced down the vomit. Morbror Vilhelm, too, put his hand over his mouth.

"That ham reminds me of something," he said. "Those maggots make me think of . . . well, just now I can't remember what they make me think of."

We stared at the maggots. They tried to squirm back into their ham. They were fat. They pushed each other to get back into their ham. But the rotten meat had fallen apart. Morbror Vilhelm went outside to vomit.

"Your putrid ham makes me think of Sweden, mor," he said when he came back. "That's what it reminded me of! And the maggots are us. Fat, bloated Swedes trying to squirm back into something that no longer exists. Back into a rotten outmoded society."

"Ah, Vilhelm!"

"Yes, yes! Only we don't realize that our ham is rotten. That it stinks! No more do these overfed maggots, who try to squirm back into their ham, their country." Morbror Vilhelm put his hand over his mouth, as if he wanted to throw up again.

————

"Won't it be exciting to meet royalty?" mor said.

"Royalty?"

"Have your forgotten Agnes has asked you to her children's party? To meet the little princesses? Remember to curtsy deeply. But not too deeply. Don't stare at the princesses. And just nibble at the refreshments."

"May I go skating, mor?"

"Don't mind Edit," laughed Maud. "She's daft."

"Skating!" cried mor. "At this moment? You do try my patience, Edit. You live in a world of your own. Other girls would give anything to meet our little princesses, whose photographs fill our weeklies. Princess Märta, Princess Astrid! Get dressed!"

A red carpet was laid across the snowy pavement outside the apartment house where my friend lived. "It's because royalty is coming," said Hanna.

"Royalty?"

"The princesses, for heaven's sake! Have you already forgotten?"

35

Hanna had brought me to the children's party because mor said dangerous men out of work roamed
the streets. I didn't see any. Ragged boys with running noses stood beyond the red carpet, sticking out
their tongues at the girls in their party dresses. "Shit-
brats!" a boy shouted at us. He looked just like Holger! He had long yellow hair like Holger's. I wanted to
play with him.

"Fuck-brat!" I shouted back at him.

"Child, I'll fetch you at six," said Hanna. "Don't
eat as if you didn't get enough food at home."

"We don't," I said.

I made a beeline for the table with pastry on it.
No one was looking. I wolfed a jam tart, a chocolate
roll, a cream puff. I ran to the toilet, threw up. When I
got back, more girls had arrived; I joined them for a
second feed. I felt happy! I ate more cream puffs, more
jam tarts. Agnes's mother had pearls around her neck.
She sat down at the piano. All the girls, except me,
sang. Mor had said my pitch was bad! I felt suddenly
unhappy.

Ping, ping, ping! Hurrah! Six o'clock. I flung myself into the hallway where servants waited for their
charges.

"Hanna!" I pulled her away. "Come on, Hanna!"

The street boys still hung about round the red carpet. They were ashen with cold. The one I liked, the
one who looked like Holger, called me "shit-brat"
again. "Fuck-fart!" I replied.

"Let me stay and play with him, Hanna. Just ten
minutes."

She pulled me away. "You'd get your hair full of
lice! You'd catch their germs. Don't you hear them
cough? Well, were the princesses nice? At your
party?"

"Oh, were there princesses at the party, Hanna?"

"Your sisters are right," Hanna said. "You're daft, Edit. You're daft."

———

Mor sat looking into the fire.

"Dance the polka, mor?"

"We're going out! Put on your snowboots."

"It's Christmas next week," mor said on the street. "But we're not giving each other presents this year, child. We're giving things to the poor instead."

"I want a pair of skates."

"They want bread! Hanna's crazy niece told Elsa that the workers starve in Stockholm. I had no idea. It seems it is the reason there are so many strikes. Oh, I don't understand these things," sighed mor. "I thought no one starved in Sweden."

"I'm scared, mor!"

"I am scared, too," mor said. We'd begun to climb toward the slums of Söder. They stunk of shit. Mor shuddered. "How human beings can live in such conditions!" she said.

Behind a wooden fence was a shack. A woman opened the door. She didn't curtsy to mor. Once mor had told me about the horse buses that existed in Stockholm when she was a girl. One day a bus-horse had skidded on the ice, had fallen down, had broken his legs: the bus driver had whipped him to get to his feet. The horse had looked at mor as he was being whipped. He couldn't get up. The woman in the doorway looked at mor, too.

"I got your name from a charity organization that

helps needy families," smiled mor. "I'm bringing you some Christmas sausages." She handed a paper bag to the woman. "May we come in a moment and thaw out, Fru Karlson?"

"No!"

"No?"

"Our strike failed today, frun. The strike funds gave out. Last week my husband was beaten over the head by the military. Yesterday he was run down by a mounted officer! But my husband went on with our strike. He only gave up this morning!"

Fru Karlson opened the door wider so we could see inside, where somebody hung on a hook. Mor shrieked. I wanted to run away, but mor grabbed my hand, pinned my hand in hers. She stared at the striker on his hook. He stared at her.

I tried to tear myself free once again, but mor's hand clutched mine and would not let go.

"Is he . . . dead?" I asked.

"Dead, indeed," Fru Karlson said. "The police are on their way over to cut him down. He died for our strike! When the strike failed, he failed."

She threw mor's bag of sausages in the snow.

"Charitable ladies didn't give a penny to our strike fund!" she said. "Now that our strike has failed, you come round and dole out charity. Keep your charity sausages. My dead husband can't eat them." Fru Karlson spat in the snow. "Ladies. You and your likes." She went back into her shack, slammed the door in mor's face. Snow poured down on us. The paper bag got covered up with snow. A sausage stuck out. It looked like a finger pointing at us.

———

"It's Saturday, Greta, Elsa, Maud," I cried. *"Saturday!"*

No one answered me. No one ever answered me. "I'm all packed," I told everyone.

I ran from room to room, my sponge bag in my hand, my snowcap on my head. But everyone was busy. Hanna snored in the kitchen, the beauties filed their nails. Mor in her sofa sat staring into the fire. Since our trip to Söder, she no longer played the piano; she just sat staring into her fire. I'd asked Elsa what was wrong. She'd answered, "Oh, something. Leave mor alone."

"We'll be late," I told mor, but she didn't answer me. She didn't look at me. I bent down; I sniffed at mor: she no longer smelled of roses.

"Aren't we off to the sauna?" I asked her.

"Sauna?" said mor. "Oh, the sauna," and got up.

In the street, the five of us hurried ahead in the dark. We arrived, tore off our clothes, dashed to the scrub room.

"Mind you scrub yourself," my sister Greta said.

"Mind, mind," laughed the beauties. "Must, must. Do, don't. Pet words of yours, Greta."

"I like to scrub myself," I said.

Greta never paid any attention to me. Everything bored my eldest sister except irregular verbs. She didn't like anything except irregular German words, irregular French verbs. But now, suddenly, she looked at me.

"You like to scrub yourself? You like to be clean, Edit?"

"I like to be clean. I'll scrub your back," I said, and she padded over to where I stood. "I'll scrub yours," she said. All at once, I liked Greta. Greta liked me.

"Come to the hot room," shouted the beauties.

It was late. Most sauna bathers had gone home. The five of us lay sweating out the week's dirt. Then we dived into the cold-water pool. Then the bath attendants whipped us with birch switches to get up our circulation.

"Now back into the pool," the attendant cried.

But she told us that we swam too wildly, splashed each other too wildly, made too much noise. I splashed more. I made more noise. I banged into my sisters in the waves we'd stirred up. I thought I'd die from happiness. I always thought I might die from happiness in water.

"We'll race," cried mor.

I stared at her. Mor looked like herself again. I sniffed her. She smelled of roses. The happy water had done that to mor. We lined up at the edge of the pool before diving.

"Five young does!" said a bath attendant. The five of us jumped in, raced. I knew I'd win. In water games, I always won. I won this time, too. We got out of the pool. We jumped in again.

"Get out," shouted the bath attendant. "It's late! We're closing."

"You've been in the water an hour, girls," she said. "What would your mother say if she knew?"

"*She's* our mother!" I laughed, pointing to mor.

"That child?" said the bath attendant. "She's their mother," she told the second attendant.

"That child?" said the second attendant.

The five of us ran home in the dark. We smelled of clean water. The snow beat down on us. We smelled of clean snow.

———

That Sunday mor said, "All of you, please come to church with me." She seldom went herself. "All of you," she repeated.

In church people stunk of sour winter coats. I pinched my nose. I always dozed off in church, but that Sunday I did something I'd never done in church: I stayed awake. I thought. I'd never thought before! At least, I'd never known that I thought. It was nice to know I was thinking. I looked at mor, who sat next to me. I thought about her. Mor sat staring at Christ, who'd always hung where he hung today, but she looked at him as if she'd never seen him before. The woman on my other side began to stink of sour winter coat. I pinched my nose harder. I gazed at Christ on his cross, dozed off.

I dreamt that I was looking at the striker who'd hung on his hook. I woke up. I rubbed my eyes. The striker on his hook wasn't there. In front of me Christ hung on his cross, as he'd done whenever mor had taken us to church. I yawned. I looked at mor to see if she, too, was asleep. But mor sat gaping at Christ on his cross just the way she'd gaped at the striker on his hook.

———

Our history teacher had got a boil on her bottom, she couldn't sit down. Professor Lithner took over. She sat looking at our class. She yawned so violently that one could look deep into her throat. She was a famous professor.

"What date is it today?" she asked, yawning again.

"The seventeenth of March," she answered herself. "To you it's just another day. Yet it is a histo-ri-cal day. Somewhere on our planet, a historical event is taking place. An era is coming to an end somewhere. Or a new era is beginning—somewhere. Somewhere in the world a seed, that will bear fruit, is being planted today. Remember: each day the seed of a great event is planted in fertile earth."

She closed her eyes. She sat thinking for a long time. She opened her eyes, but when she caught sight of our class, she began to yawn with such boredom that I was afraid her jaws would break.

"What does history mean to girls like you?" she asked.

"Kings," answered Agnes. "Wars."

"Wars and kings?" Fröken Lithner asked. She looked at Agnes, yawned again. "Who are Sweden's greatest kings? According to you?" she asked of Agnes. "According to you?"

"Gustavus Adolphus of the Thirty Years War. And Charles the Twelfth," Agnes answered, and Fröken Lithner told everyone who shared Agnes's historical opinions to raise their hand.

"What's wrong with those monarchs?" she asked of me. I was the only one who hadn't raised my hand.

"They were shits," I said.

The class tittered. Fröken Lithner stopped yawning. She turned away from the rest of the class. She sat gazing at me: "What's your name?" she asked.

"Edit."

"Edit—what?"

"Toll."

"Your military family wouldn't agree with your unorthodox point of view. Not the field marshal anyway! Field Marshal Toll—if he were alive. So what's wrong with those monarchs?" she asked me. "What's wrong with them?" She had stopped yawning.

"They let Swedish children die in the snow with tufts of hay in their mouths," I answered.

Fröken Lithner stared at me. She heaved herself up. "I'm due at a teachers' meeting." She began to move heavily toward the door, as if she was dragging a sack of potatoes.

"Tomorrow your own history teacher will be back with you," she said, sounding relieved. She stopped at my desk. Suddenly she opened her sleepy eyes. Her eyes looked like lamps with the wicks turned up very high.

"Tufts of hay, eh?" she said. "Tufts of hay, Edit Toll!"

———

Winters, summers, ran in, ran out. Suddenly my three sisters had grown six breasts. Elsa's, Greta's, were like big snowballs.

"Yours are small," I told Maud.

"They're my despair," wailed Maud. She had stood on her head to make them grow. "I've heard that helps," she said.

My three sisters had got blond hair on their stomachs. They bled once a month.

"Why, mor?" I asked.

"Child, it's not a nice thing to talk about. It has to do with growing up. Growing up isn't . . . nice!" mor said. "We don't talk about growing up."

43

Mor never told me anything. My sisters never told me anything. In school no one ever told us anything. We didn't know that no one ever told us anything. We didn't know that we didn't know anything. But I felt as if I had a hole inside me: a know-nothing-hole. I began to fill it with reading. I began to devour *The Eddas.* The Icelandic sagas of eight hundred years ago became more real to me than the year I lived in. The Edda people seemed more alive than the people who surrounded me. Oh! The Edda people laughed, wept, shouted, danced, killed, swam across lakes, skied down mountains, slew each other, loved each other!

"Eat your *Edda Sagas,* why don't you? Chew them!" laughed the beauties. "Edit is daft," they told each other. "Still daft," they said. And then they ran off. They were always running off to parties. "La-la," they sang when they left. "La-la," they sang when they came back. And again they laughed. They looked at each others' beautiful bodies as they undressed, laughed again, jumped into their beds, blew out our petrol lamp.

"I'm reading," I cried.

"Oh, are you awake?" laughed the beauties. "One never notices. You're so insignificant." They laughed again. They fell asleep. They began to breathe softly. They began to snore softly. They slept in the moon-light with their long hair for quilts.

———

Agnes's father was sent abroad as military attaché. I had to make new friends. I had never had friends who were "commoners" before, but they accepted me. They were kind; they took an interest in the stories I wrote. I illustrated them with crayons. "May we keep your stories?" they asked.

Oh! How I wrote. How I drew. Everyone wanted my funny stories. My evenings weren't long enough to fill the orders that came in. I began to illustrate my stories during class, never listening to what the teachers said. I drew everything I didn't own myself, everything I'd seen in magazines: lovely clothes, satin slippers, soft beds with silk covers. I drew "bad" women. I had seen one in an advertisement for perfume.

"Who's she?" I'd asked mor.

"A bad woman," shuddered mor. She threw the magazine into the fire. I had liked the bad woman. Soon all my women looked liked her. They clutched glasses of champagne in their manicured fingers. Their shoulder straps slid off, showing breasts as big as big snowballs.

"Edit!"

I hadn't heard our teacher. I was drawing a tit with a strawberry for nipple.

"I'm speaking to you, Edit."

I added a cigarette to my bad woman's mouth, added a green navel with my green crayon. I laughed. Oh! I'd like to have a green navel!

My neighbor nudged me: "Fröken is speaking to you, Edit," she whispered.

Shit. I hadn't finished my illustration.

"Bring me your drawing," said fröken.

I got up, I crossed the classroom, looked at fröken. Heavens, she was ugly. She grabbed my drawing, gasped.

"Go to the principal. Show her this . . . foul

thing. You will be expelled. Are you listening, Edit? Have you as much as heard what I'm telling you?" she shouted at me.

I shook my head. I had heard, vaguely, something about being expelled. Something about being expelled? But just then I decided I'd put violets between my bad woman's manicured toes—it'd looked terribly funny. Fröken looked wild.

"How many girls have you given this . . . this sort of abomination?" she asked. She looked angry.

"Oh, I'd say all my friends. Everyone in our class," I answered. Everyone tittered.

"Class dismissed," screamed fröken. She was beside herself. Her moustaches had begun to tremble. I took a close look at them. I always looked at things very closely. But fröken shouted: "Go! Go!"

———

My sisters had been confirmed.

"One day it will be your turn," mor said ecstatically.

"My turn for what?" I asked, looking up from my *Edda Saga.* I yawned. Mor always spoke of such dull things. "My turn for what, mor?"

"To get confirmed. To confirm your faith in God," mor answered.

"*Faith?*"

"Child, how can I explain faith to you?" mor said. "Look, when you travel on a train, you have faith in the train conductor. Don't you? Complete faith? The faith we Christians have in God."

"A train conductor drove his train off the rails last

week. He was drunk. Everyone was killed." I hooted with laughter. I thought of a funny drawing I'd make of God, steering a train off the rails, drunk as a Lord.

Mor stared at me. "How can you laugh at such serious things as . . . God? As faith?" she asked. She'd begun to weep. "Aren't you ever afraid?"

"No, mor."

She threw her hands—her small white gloves—before her face. I wanted to kiss them, I wanted to kiss mor, to love mor. But the drawing of God I saw in my imagination, steering his train off the rails, drunk as a Lord, was hilarious. I just had to laugh. Mor threw herself down in her sofa.

"Go to your room, Edit. Stay there!" she sobbed. "Oh, I never want to see you again. I don't want to hear you laugh again. Your cruel little-girl laughter. Your pagan laughter."

"Oh! Mor!"

"Leave me!"

———

Farbror Karl glittered in his general's uniform under the chandeliers. He was entertaining the family. We curtsied to him, passed into the other drawing room, joining the other Tolls at the family party.

"Good day, Axel."

"Good day, Edit."

"Good day, Brita."

"Good day, Edit."

"Good day, Gustaf!"

"Good day, Edit."

47

We were all Tolls. All family. Farbror Johann, who was the stupidest of all the Tolls, was also the head of the family. He was the baron. When he died, his son, Erik, would be the baron. If more Tolls died, my father would become the baron. In the meanwhile, we were all "honorables." Honorable Greta, Elsa, Maud, Edit Toll.

"Good day, Farbror Johann."

"Good day, Edit."

There were dozens of Tolls to greet. I skipped some, edged my way to the buffet. "I always eat as simply as my soldiers," Farbror Karl used to say. "And as much," he'd laugh.

I ate as much as a soldier of Farbror Karl's. I was hungry. I wolfed pies, sausage, gazing across my heaped plate at Farbror Karl who (as we had no father) supervised our bringing up. I behaved differently with Farbror Karl than I did with all other people; I never laughed in his presence. I stood as straight as one of his officers when he spoke to me. I seldom listened to what anyone told me, but I listened to every word Farbror Karl said. Once I'd met him riding in Djurgarden, holding two batons in his hand, the baton that all generals must carry, and a second baton because he was also commander of the town of Stockholm.

"Is Farbror Karl very clever?" I'd asked of Greta. "He has got two batons!"

"He's not clever," Greta had answered. "He's honest. He's reliable. He's sincere. He's a . . . great man."

She'd stared before her.

"Those qualities are superior to a slick brain. Sweden trusts Farbror Karl the way Sweden trusted his father. He was marshal at the Royal Court. He too, was reliable, truthful, sincere. Toll virtues, all."

"Does far have Toll virtues?"

"He has a slick brain. Far laughs at Farbror Karl's virtues. But where is our father now? Nowhere. He's a clever nonentity," said Greta with anger. "I am glad that mor divorced him when we were small."

That night at the family party, Farbror Karl came up to me. I was still wolfing food in my corner.

"You're hungry?" he asked.

"I'm always hungry, Farbror Karl."

"So I see," he smiled. His face was a strong, truthful face. I longed to throw myself into his arms.

"How are you getting on at school, Edit?"

"Badly, Farbror Karl."

"Then do better. The family's helping to pay expensive school fees for you and your sisters. You're attending Sweden's foremost girls' school, Edit. At eighteen, you'll have to pass the stiffest examinations of any school in any country. Sweden's standards are high. But you must pass. Without your certificate, you won't find acceptable work. You must find work. You four sisters are penniless. Edit, will you give me your word that you'll work harder from now on?"

"No, Farbror Karl."

"No?"

I wasn't intimidated by the great general, I wasn't intimidated by the commander of the city of Stockholm. But I was sick at heart at disappointing Farbror Karl. Yet I knew that I'd never work hard at anything I didn't love. I wouldn't promise Farbror Karl something I knew I wouldn't keep.

I repeated: "No, Farbror Karl."

His blue eyes looked into mine. "You don't like to lie, do you, Edit?"

"I don't like to lie."

He laid his hand on my shoulder: the hand into which our country had placed two batons because Far-

4 9

bror Karl was . . . honest. He smiled down at me. I smiled back. And all at once I knew that I'd never forget that exchange of smiles. Not as long as I lived!

"Eat, child," he said. "You're very thin. Eat."

Farbror Karl went back to his duties as a host. His face was as bright as the candles in the chandeliers that shone on his blue uniform, as he moved among the members of the Toll family.

"Mor just sits," I said to Elsa.

"She's praying."

"She's praying to Countess Hamilton's God," Elsa said. She explained that Tant Marie-Louise Hamilton had become a close friend of mor's. "Overnight, almost," Elsa said. As always, she was brushing her gold hair. A star shone on it. All at once, she stopped brushing.

"It seems that one day mor saw a striking worker hanging on a hook," she said.

"It shook her." Elsa sighed. I'd never heard her sigh before. "In that moment of strong emotions, mor could have become a person. She was so upset that for once she wanted to do something. But she had the bad luck to run into Tant Marie-Louise Hamilton a few minutes later. On the street. Countess Hamilton invited her to tea that very afternoon.

"And she told Mor the dead striker had been a bad man. 'All strikers are bad,' Tant Marie-Louise said. But for once mor was stubborn. She said she wanted to do something for the poor of Stockholm. Mor hadn't known, she told Tant Marie-Louise, that

Swedish workers starved, but the countess assured her that God looked after them.

" 'He doesn't want us to meddle,' the countess said. 'God knows what is best for the poor. We're not supposed to interfere with his designs. We're not asked to do anything except to pray. My dear, pray! It'll ease your scruples. And please come for tea this afternoon.' "

"Did mor tell you . . . all that?"

"She told me all that nonsense, yes. Since then she's done nothing but sit on her sofa praying."

Elsa stopped talking. She looked at the star above the roof opposite, and she no longer brushed her hair. Elsa liked to think. And every year she seemed to like it more than the year before.

"It doesn't sound as if you like mor," I said.

"I don't. I adore mor. She is a woman of such enormous inner nobility. Vulgarity of mind—she doesn't know what it means. Insincerity, vanity, absence of generosity—all those things are as abhorrent to mor's heart as a poisonous mushroom would be to her delicate little stomach.

"Edit," Elsa suddenly asked me, "have you ever seen a deformed foot?"

She came closer to my bed.

"An ill-fitting boot can give a foot bunions and calluses. It can cause malformations of the bone as well. Mor's mind is a deformed foot," said Elsa. "And far was the boot that deformed it. It wasn't far's fault. The fault lay with the . . . the mentality of his kin, with the prejudices of our clan. And now a hypocritic hag like Countess Hamilton will keep mor's poor little mind deformed forever. Mor has turned to God like all mentally crippled oldsters."

"Oldsters? Mor?"

51

"Everyone who resorts to superstitions is old. Mor is leaning very heavily on the crutch of a nonexistent God, on a crutch called religion. Mor's mind has become calloused with the bunions of superstition, the bunions of fear, the bunions of prejudice . . .

"I love mor!"

"I adore her," Elsa said again.

The star that had illuminated her gold hair had slid off. She jumped into bed.

———

Was there a war? A war! Outside of Sweden?

No one spoke of it, and in school we studied the old wars of Sweden's many Karls, the old wars of France's many Louis. The only person who stormed against the present war was Hanna's niece, Gärda.

"Moster Hanna, it has arrived, the world war plotted by criminals, lauded by lunatics, carried out by slaves," shouted Gärda, but deaf Hanna just snored away beside her stove. "Speaker Zeth Höglund told us that at tonight's meeting." Then she dashed off to her job at Grand Hotel.

"Mor's got a bee in her bonnet," Maud said one day. The war had gone on for a long time. Now it had crept closer to Sweden. But it didn't bother Maud.

"Besides God, I mean," she giggled.

"Well, what's mor's new 'bee'?" Greta asked.

"Bringing sandwiches to the trains with the wounded soldiers who're coming from Russia and who are going home to Germany," Maud said.

She told us that all the elegant Stockholm ladies

knitted wool caps for the kaiser's soldiers, and delivered them in person at our Central Station.

"Any Swede who counts is pro-German," said Maud. "Mor apes them! Schs-ss! Here she comes. Dressed warmly for her little outing."

"It's eight o'clock," mor said. "Edit, I'd like you to come along with me. The train with the wounded soldiers arrives at eight thirty."

"I don't want to come, mor."

"I want you to come."

Mor took my hand. I snatched it away. I was too old to be held by the hand. One's hand was one's property. But when we arrived at the Central Station, I saw lots and lots of hands, reaching out from the open windows of the train carriages. Those hands reached out for the sandwiches the charitable Stockholm ladies had brought.

I threw a look at the wounded soldiers in the lit-up carriage windows, but they didn't interest me. What did interest me was the look of hatred in their eyes. They stared at the charitable Stockholm ladies sneeringly, and one boy with a bloody bandage round his head stuck out his tongue at them.

I couldn't help laughing. Mor grabbed my hand again: this time she pinned my hand in hers.

I asked mor, pointing, "Who travels in that carriage, mor?" The curtains of the carriage were drawn. No voices came out of it.

"Those are the basket cases," murmured mor.

"Basket cases?"

"Boys without arms or legs, small enough to fit into a basket. Small enough to be shipped home in . . . little baskets."

I pulled my hand away so violently that mor almost toppled over on the station platform.

"I hate it," I cried.

"What—oh *war*? Yes, wars are awful. But necessary. Tant Hedvig told me the king told her—they played bridge—that monarchs couldn't dominate their unruly masses without war."

I ran off, I dashed away from the station, mor like a whirlwind behind me. She caught up with me. She grabbed my hand again, and I bent down and bit her fingers. On my face was the hatred I'd seen on the wounded soldiers' faces when they jeered at the charitable ladies.

"Don't ever dare to grab my hand again!" I shouted to mor. "Don't dare drag me along to see things I don't want to see. Don't you dare. Don't you dare!"

At that moment I hated mor. I hated her for knitting caps for heads that were covered with blood instead of hair. I hated her for bringing chopped-meat sandwiches to boys who were nothing but chopped meat themselves.

"Fuck-ass!" I told mor inside my face. "Shit-fart."

I burst into tears. I loved mor. I loved her nose. I loved her hands, which she pressed to her cheeks, which looked like small white gloves.

Docilely I went home with mor, my outside-face weeping because I'd hurt the only person I loved in the world. But behind my face, those soldiers' looks of hatred grew into a sneer as deep as theirs. And I knew that contempt was engraved on my inside-face forever. Forever and ever and ever.

———

54

"We haven't got an extra bed, Greta," cried mor. But Greta answered that everyone in Stockholm must put up a peasant for three nights. "It is a patriotic duty," she said.

As always she sounded annoyed with mor.

"We'll invite the peasant allotted to us in for a cup of acorn coffee," mor answered.

She clasped her small hands in ecstasy.

"It's so beautiful. Thirty thousand peasants traveling all the way to Stockholm to tell our King Gustaf that they are loyal to him. It is an extraordinary event."

"You're wrong. As usual," Greta corrected mor. "It's a historical tradition," she informed us. "Sweden's peasantry has always rallied around their monarch in times of danger."

"Have you heard the awful news?" Greta asked us later. "Stockholm's workers are staging a counter-rally. Today! While the king speaks to his faithful peasants in the palace yard. At three o'clock, fifty thousand factory workers will hold an antiwar demonstration outside the palace. Not that Sweden is in danger of war. She's in danger from her organized labor hordes."

Greta marched toward the door. "Sweden's loyal peasants must feel very proud today," she said. "And excited."

Our peasant wasn't excited.

He just sat and stank. He dunked his black wartime bread in his acorn coffee: burped, farted. Mor moved quickly out of his way.

"You must feel so thrilled," she said.

"Eh?" He put his hand behind his ear. "I don't hear anything."

"I said that you must be . . . so . . . thrilled,"

mor said. "It must be so glorious for all of you peasants having your king ask for your protection. You will help him? You will put down the rebellious factory hands?"

"Eh?"

Mor's peasant was deafer even than our Hanna. He put his two hands behind both of his ears that had dirty tufts of hair nestling in them.

"I don't know why I am in Stockholm," he said. "I don't know why they nabbed me. In my village, no one knew why they were nabbed. We were just planting our spring potatoes. I'm going home."

"Home? But you've only just come," said mor. "You must be in the palace yard at three o'clock."

She went as close to her stink-peasant as she dared: "His Majesty will speak to you from his balcony. At three. He'll ask you for money with which to build a warship. Against the Russians," cried mor ecstatically. But her peasant had got up. He put on his sheepskin cap. He took his railway ticket from his worn pocket and gaped at it upside down. For the first time he looked happy.

"I'm going now," he said. "To the railway station. Tomorrow I'll plant my potatoes. I don't know why they made us come to Stockholm. None of us know. Well, they paid our fare. Thank you for the coffee, frun," he said, and her peasant stomped off.

I laughed; mor sobbed.

"A real peasant," wept mor, wringing her hands. "A semi-idiot."

I had liked the peasant. He had stunk just like Nilson in Sjögård. But mor hadn't liked his smell. She threw open the windows of her drawing room to get rid of it. "Peasants are horrid," she wept. "Just as horrid as the horrid factory workers."

"I can't swallow another bite!"

"Very well, if you don't know how to behave, leave the table," Greta said. "Members of the lower classes complain when they are in difficult situations. Upper-class people don't. That's one of the many differences between upper and lower classes. Finish your mackerel in your room."

"Mor," I began.

"Child, do what Greta bids you," murmured mor. She didn't like to be hard. But Greta was strong and mor was weak. She kept her eyes lowered.

Three pairs of stern eyes stared at me with distaste as I left the dining room. The eyes of my sisters said I was not up to standard. Even Maud, who like me was scraggy from growing too fast on too little food, was able to control the rumblings of her hungry stomach. Maud was silly; she was stupid. But her manners were Toll.

I sat down on my bed. As I stared at the mackerel on my plate, I remembered yesterday's newspaper photo of a torpedoed sailor floating down the west coast of Sweden, where drowned British and German sailors arrived, daily, by the hundreds. On the newspaper photo, a mackerel swum out of the sailor's eye, which had been plucked empty by sea gulls.

I sat picking at the mackerel with my fork. Had it grown fat on some sailor's eyeballs, I wondered. A slimy piece came off: vomit filled my mouth. Yet, if I didn't eat my mackerel, it would be served me tomorrow, the day after, and the day after. We were a military family. Orders were orders. And no one would speak to me till I'd eaten my foul fish. I would be considered an outcast. Not a Toll!

57

I attacked the fish, but it'd begun to stink of dead sailor's eyeballs. I couldn't sit all evening in our unheated bedroom. I began to cough. My school uniform was thin from too-long wear; it had come down to me from Greta, from Elsa, from Maud. I peered down at it. It looked mildewy. I shook from the cold; I didn't know what to do next. If I hadn't finished my food before my three sisters came to bed, they'd blow out the kerosene lamp and go to sleep without a glance in the direction of the outcast. They'd let me sit in the chill moonlight throughout the night, with the congealed mackerel on my plate. In their eyes I'd no longer "belong."

I gobbled the mackerel. I fled to the toilet. I vomited up the sailor's eyeballs.

———

It was my turn to serve tea at mor's weekly evening.

"I'll brush your hair two hundred times if you take my place tonight," I told Elsa. "I hate it."

"The four of us hate mor's evenings," Elsa said. "Tonight's your turn. Besides I want to finish a Strindberg novel, while mor's busy with her cronies."

Elsa groaned. "Mor still forbids me to read the world's greatest writer because he's an outspoken antimilitarist. And because he scoffs at riches and titles. Besides she can't bear his calling married women parasites because they live off their husbands." Elsa sounded upset. "Our mor has never done a stroke of work in her life. Nor have her friends." She gave me a friendly shove. "Now go and serve tea, Edit."

I pulled mor's tea trolley into the drawing room, curtsied three times: once to Tant Maja von Göes, once to Tant Hedvig von Feilitzen, once to Countess Hamilton.

"The king told me . . ." said Tant Hedvig, and I yawned behind my face. For an hour I'd be hearing, "The king told me . . . ," for Tant Hedvig never spoke of anyone except His Majesty. And I had to be in attendance till nine o'clock. It was barely eight. "When I played bridge last night at the palace, the king told me . . ."

"Did you hold good hands, Hedvig?"

"Let me finish, Marie-Louise. What was I saying? I've lost my thread. Ah, yes, His Majesty has come out strongly for capital punishment!" Tant Hedvig stirred her linden tea in one of Grandmother Horn's transparent china cups. "Naturally, I agree with him. I always agree with His Majesty," she smiled.

Mor nodded. "I always agree with you, Hedvig."

"Then you're for capital punishment? Like His Majesty. Good. Branting wants to do away with capital punishment. He should hang!"

(Hang?)

Hanna's niece said that when they hanged prisoners they wept like babies and, once dead, their tongues stuck out like overstuffed sausages. But Tant Hedvig liked hangings? Mor liked hangings?

"Look out, Edit!"

I'd dropped Tant Hedvig's teacup. I hurried off for a dish towel. When I came back, mor and her friends were chatting happily about other things.

"There's nothing wrong with war profiteering," Tant Maja von Göes said, while I wiped up the spilt tea. She sounded excited. "My husband has explained

59

to me why businessmen stockpile. The war won't last forever, you see. Of course, it's too bad that our population doesn't get enough to eat, but business is business. Sweden's big businessmen have hoarded enormous quantities of wheat and potatoes. It makes prices rise. That's the moment to sell. Our business wizards do sell. At soaring prices," smiled Tant Maja, looking at her diamond ring.

Mor's nose had got white. She threw me a wild look. "Go to bed, Edit. You must be in school at eight," she said. Her little voice sounded pinched. She threw her three friends a nervous glance, but Tant Maja, Tant Hedvig, Tant Marie-Louise were already cackling away about something else, just like hens in a poultry yard.

I dropped three deep curtsies. I kissed mor's hand. I ran off, I jumped into bed. Capital punishment? War profiteering? I pulled the blanket over my head.

———

Hanna's swollen legs made her a prisoner in the cell of her kitchen: once a year she coaxed them out of doors. "Hulda's nameday, Edit!"

This year she said, "Hulda has baked a cake, child. Do you want to come along?"

I shouted: "A cake!" Maud cried, "I'll come along!"

In the street Maud began to run. "Let's hurry. By the time we get there, Hulda'll have gobbled up her cake."

"You bad girl. You never trust anyone. You judge

60

everyone after you own wicked self," Hanna said. "You are mean. That's why you think everyone else is mean, too." Hanna tried to keep up with Maud and me. "I've known Hulda for forty years. All the years I worked for my countess, she worked for her baroness."

"Did you work for a countess, Hanna?" I asked.

"You're daft, Edit," said Hanna. "I worked for your farmor. Oh, girls, don't run. My legs are swollen twice normal size."

I wished mine were. The street boys still cried "rooster legs," still threw snowballs at my legs. But this afternoon there weren't many street boys about; it was twenty below zero. Only poor schoolchildren were doing their homework beneath the lit-up street-lamps. "They'll soon be dead," Hanna said. "Children die fast in wartime. Listen to them coughing."

"You shut up," shouted Maud.

Maud looked ill. Her bones were hollow—like mine. Sweden's queen was German. All food went to Germany. We hadn't had meat, butter, sugar, white flour for years, not even potatoes. Only rutabagas and mackerel. Maud's digestion had got so bad that she groaned after every meal; her hair had begun to fall out.

"Welcome to my little nameday party," cried Hulda from her window.

We dashed in from the cold. Hulda's room, like everyone else's, was unheated, but she had put red tissue paper round her lamp: it made her room glow like a rose in summer. "Keep your coats on," she said, "and your snowcaps. And your overboots."

"Many heartfelt congratulations on your name-day, dear Hulda," Hanna said.

We sat down in a row on the sofa. Hulda heated

coffee made from acorns: her room stunk of roasted acorns.

"The cake," Maud hissed in my ear. "It was a lie? Cake in wartime! I knew it was a lie."

The coffee kept bubbling on the stove, Hulda and Hanna talked of old days: "My countess said . . ." "My baroness said . . ." Only their two dead mistresses counted for them. Hulda and Hanna sounded just like the coffeepot that was bubbling away on the fire.

"I've saved three months' sugar rations so that I might bake a cake for you, Hanna dear," Hulda said. She smiled at Hanna. Hanna smiled at her old friend.

"Hulda, your cake isn't sweetened with sugar," said Hanna. "It's sweetened with love. You have deprived yourself of sugar for three months? For my sake! Yes, yes, your cake is sweetened with love, Hulda."

"Love," hissed Maud in my ear. "Love!"

Green sugar-leaves danced round Hulda's frosted cake, holding red sugar-hearts by the hand. It was the prettiest cake I'd ever seen. Hulda cut it. She handed each of us a chunk. I ate half of mine, I shoved the other half into my pocket to eat later. Maud gobbled all of hers, turned pea green because of her terrible digestion.

"Let go of me, you devils," someone shouted in the street. "She-devils!"

We ran to the window. But it was only a policeman warding off women who were trying to get into an empty food shop.

"There's nothing in the shops today," Hulda told us. "Not even sea gulls. Nor squirrels. Hedgehogs, too, are sold out."

"Hulda, I'm thankful that my countess is dead,"

said Hanna. "I wouldn't have served my countess hedgehogs for anything. Ah, it's all the fault of the war."

"No, it's the fault of the socialists," Hulda said.

"Sch-ss," said Hanna. "Don't talk to them in front of the children, Hulda."

"Now we shall have to leave," Hanna said. "There are dangerous people on the streets these days. Famished children! They'd do murder for a piece of bread. They'd stick a knife into one for a potato."

Hulda passed her hand over Maud's silver-fair hair. "War children," she sighed. "Getting a bit bald on top, eh?" she said, and Maud tore herself away. "Hanna, I read in the paper this morning that the hair of little girls is falling out in tufts. And if they survive, they'll have no milk in their breasts when they grow up."

Hulda shouldn't have mentioned breasts. Maud's small tennis balls were her despair. Would they ever grow big, would they ever have milk? she asked me.

Now she dashed to the door. I dashed after her. But when I reached the street, I ran upstairs again. I threw myself into Hulda's arms.

"Your cake's the best cake I've tasted in all my life, Hulda!"

———

I caught up with Maud on the black street. I shoved my piece of cake into her fist.

"Eat it! It's made with real sugar, it'll help you get milk."

Maud had never bothered with me. I bored her. I

was four years younger than she was. She never spoke to me. But now she grabbed my cake, wolfed it down, then she grabbed my hand; and as we began to run in the dark, something happened to our hands: they began to like one another. Hulda's and Hanna's world, mor's world, Greta's and Elsa's world, even, had nothing to do with ours. We were war children!

As we passed a streetlamp ringed about with coughing children doing their homework, Maud and I stopped. We looked at them. They looked at us. Maud and I belonged with them, they belonged with us. We began to hurry homeward in the black night, holding hands. We crossed an empty lot where the wind howled, "war!"

"War, war, war," howled the wind.

———

Gärda had no need to breathe. Gärda didn't need to open, nor to close her lips: words poured through the hole that was her mouth.

"I've just come from a meeting in Hornsbergs Hage, Moster Hanna," she shouted.

But Hanna didn't hear. She pointed to a red carnation in Gärda's old coat, "What's that for?"

"Wear a red carnation!" shouted Gärda. "We were told at the meeting today. A red carnation is worn by the International Workers of the World! Moster Hanna, I'm giving notice. At Grand Hotel."

Notice?" asked Hanna, holding her hand behind her ear.

"Yes, the Russian archdukes pee in their beds.

The swine are too lazy to get up. In the Russia of the tzars, their valets brought their masters their piss pots. They waited till their masters had peed their fill. Then they took away the archdukes' piss pots. Archdukes! Pfui!"

Gärda's stomach jumped up, jumped down, she laughed so hard.

"They're arriving thick and fast, Moster Hanna. The princes! From Russia! They all live in the luxury suites of Grand Hotel. They swill champagne all night, all day. They've fled from their Revolution. Re-vo-lu-tion, Moster Hanna! The devil take the bloodsuckers."

Gärda got up. She sat down on the stove. It was hot. She jumped to her feet.

"Moster Hanna, the Russian workers got rid of their tormentors. We'll get rid of ours. We'll have our revolution, Moster Hanna. Zeth Höglund told us that today. In Hornsbergs Hage."

Suddenly Hanna understood every word Gärda said.

"How do the Russian gentry get over to Sweden?" she asked her niece.

The Bay of Bothnia is frozen over," Gärda explained. "The bloodsuckers arrive in sledges full of jewels, full of sable furs." Again her stomach began to hop up, hop down, laughing.

"Moster Hanna, many sledges fall through the ice. The ice in the Bay of Bothnia is thin in places. The Highnesses drown like the rats they are. The fish at the bottom of the Bay of Bothnia will soon be able to set up jewelry shops.

The fish'll sell the grand duchesses' tiaras, the grand duchesses' sables. Fuck the bloodsuckers!"

"Go and play," Hanna told me. But I stayed with

Gärda. I liked Gärda. I never understood what she was ranting about; but I enjoyed her laughing stomach. I enjoyed her fury.

"Moster Hanna, I'm off," she cried. "To the Grand Hotel. I'll be blacklisted. I won't get another job. But I'll manage. Fuck the peeing archdukes! Fuck their piss pots!" laughed Gärda.

"Run off and play," Hanna told me.

I ran to the drawing room. "Fuck the peeing archdukes!" I shouted.

"Don't make so much noise," said mor. She pressed her hands to her eyes. "Edit, don't make so much noise."

"Fuck their piss pots," I shouted.

"Write an essay on war," our new history teacher told us. "Hand it in on Monday."

"Which war, fröken?"

"The present one. Of course. Write about the poor tzar of Holy Russia. Write about our beloved ally, the German kaiser who fought for Lebensraum for our brothers, the great German people."

That evening I sat chewing my pencil, dizzy with hunger because of the war. I couldn't concentrate. But the soldiers in Russia, in France, in England, were hungrier than me. Why didn't anyone give them food? Yesterday there had been a piece in the newspaper about a soldier who'd bitten a chunk off his own arm because he'd gone crazy from starvation. He should have eaten a chunk off a dead horse instead, I thought, or a chunk from some dead soldier.

I stopped chewing my pencil. I began to write my piece on war. I called it "The Sausage Machine." I wrote it very quickly. On Monday morning I handed it in. Monday evening the telephone rang.

"Yes, Fröken Sergelius," said mor over the phone. "I'm shocked, Fröken Sergelius. Shocked!"

Edit!"

I looked up from piercing a chilblain with a sewing needle. We had no coal because of the English boycott. Our flat was as cold as an ice shed.

"You may be expelled from school," cried mor. "There's going to be a meeting to decide about you. You've written a piece extolling cannibalism."

"Cannibalism?"

"Cannibalism means that human beings eat other human beings," sobbed mor.

I explained to mor that the military killed hundreds of thousands of young men. Millions! If the generals didn't mind murdering young men, then why should they mind eating young men? "Eating young soldiers who are already dead will prevent young soldiers who are still alive from dying from hunger," I said.

"They're dying at this minute, mor," I added. "While you and I sit chatting in your drawing room."

I told mor I'd written that each battalion should pull a little sausage-machine along on wheels: after each great battle the live soldiers would collect the murdered soldiers, put them quickly through the sausage machine, eat hot, fresh sausages with mustard.

"With mustard!" giggled Maud who'd just come in. "Edit's daft, mor. Would *you* eat sausages made from young men?"

I was hungry. I was shivering from the cold in our flat. I pierced another chilblain. "If I were willing to mass murder young men, I'd be willing to eat young men. What difference does it make? But I'd never be willing to kill young men. Never!"

Mor started to weep again. "Unless you retract every word you wrote, you might be expelled from school."

"Retract, mor?"

"Retract means to take back what one has said. Or written. Retract means you state you didn't mean a word of what you wrote, Edit."

I chewed my pencil. *Retract* was a new word in my vocabulary. I didn't retract.

———

A pimple arrived in the night.

"What's a pimple doing on my nose?" I asked mor.

She looked away. "It'll disappear."

It didn't. Pimples arrived, not singly, not in pairs—in swarms. At the same time, my body grew clumsy, my hair lost its luster, my eyes theirs.

"Elsa and Maud keep laughing at me," I told mor in her sofa before the fire. I'd covered myself with the rug that had once been mor's evening cloak, and I lay pulling at the small, mauve tufts in the wool cloth. Whenever we sisters felt like weeping, we curled up in mor's sofa and covered ourselves with "sad-coat." Pulling at the little wool-tufts made us feel better.

"Mor, tell Maud not to laugh at me whenever she sees me," I said.

"I have no influence over your big sisters any longer," mor sighed. "They've grown to be very hard.

Elsa is different at heart, but Maud's company is bad for her." Mor's voice shook. It always shook when she spoke of Elsa. She loved Elsa best of all of us. "Your big sisters don't love me any more."

"I love you."

"You're the only one who does," murmured mor. "You're all I have left."

But she hadn't answered my question about the pimples. Mor never answered questions. I left the drawing room. In the passage I banged into the beauties. Maud instantly began to laugh at me.

"Why do you laugh at me?" I asked.

"An ugly frog,

"Squats in a bog,

"Qua, Qua!" laughed Maud. She dropped a mock curtsy.

Elsa didn't laugh. "Come along with me, Edit," she said.

We stood looking out the window in our cold bedroom. "You're starting puberty," Elsa said.

"Puberty?"

"Mor wouldn't want me to explain it to you. Mor's a Victorian, afraid of the facts of life. She's afraid of life. Mor's never had a life. Besides she's ignorant."

Mor?"

"Mor was educated at home. In Sjögård. By an ignorant governess. Morbror Vilhelm was educated at home. By an ignorant tutor. Mor, like all her family, like all her friends, knows nothing, understands nothing."

Elsa gazed at me. Suddenly I understood why people were impressed with her. Elsa wasn't only a beauty. The look in her eyes was different from the look in other people's eyes.

"Edit, you're about to turn into a female. Puberty means that you're no longer a child. Your blood is beginning to boil. That brings pimples. It brings clumsiness, awkwardness, lack of charm."

"I'm not charming?"

"You'll remain an ugly toad for two years. Accept it. Live through it. Alone. Life is a series of rough, lonely patches, Edit. Puberty is one of them. And no one helps you through the rough patches. That's the worst of one's . . . rough patches. The lonesomeness. From now on you're on your own, toad."

She bent down. Her eyes looked into mine. All at once I loved Elsa. I wanted to throw my arms around her. But I'd become an ugly toad: no one would wish to be touched by a pimply toad.

I ran out of our room.

———

We lived at the corner of Grevturegaten and Vallhallavägen—a stone's throw from Lilyans Woods. I took to skiing into the lonely woods. If people no longer wanted me, I didn't want them. I decided to keep out of their way.

I skied, skied in the solitary woods where no one laughed at the puberty change in me. But it was rough, as Elsa'd said, to be on one's own. I plunged into something new. Although I was a bloated toad with pimples, I realized that the world around me was still beautiful. I'd never truly looked at nature before—at trees, at the snow, at the clouds. They were beautiful. I'd never looked at the magpies that winged through the snow-covered woods. They shone like black satin—beautifully.

70

I gazed at everything, as I skied deeper into the lonesome Lilyans Woods. One day I caught sight of another lonesome person in the woods—a man, and he too was skiing ahead into more lonesomeness. He stopped, took a bottle of schnaps from his pocket, drank deeply from the bottle, caught sight of me, and fled deeper into the lonesomeness of Lilyans Woods. He must feel just as lonely as if he was a pimply toad, I thought. Perhaps he had his "pimples" inside of him.

———

Hanna's niece Gärda was talking a blue streak in the kitchen. Didn't Gärda mind that Hanna couldn't hear a word? Was she talking to herself?

She was talking to Elsa.

I had never seen Elsa in the kitchen before. She was filling a glass of water at the tap, and I understood what had brought her to the kitchen. Hunger! The hungrier the war made us, the more water we drank. Elsa, listening to Gärda, sipped her water. I, too, filled a glass at the tap. The hunger pains almost stopped.

"A butcher sold a girl as hash yesterday," said Gärda, shouting for Hanna's benefit. "He's in jail, Fröken Elsa. But he says he found the girl dead from starvation on a garbage dump. I and my group think that the butcher told the truth. Fröken Elsa, we're holding a mass demonstration tonight to protest against the hunger profiteers. Sweden's black marketeers are selling food to Germany while Swedish children are found dead on garbage heaps, fröken."

"Shame!" Gärda shrieked.

She shoved a pamphlet into Elsa's hand.

"The photo on the cover is a photo of Kata, Fröken Elsa. Kata wrote this pamphlet herself. It's called 'Shame!' Kata'll be speaking tonight. I'll sell her pamphlets at the entrance of the hall. Many of us will."

"Who is Kata?" asked Elsa.

She looked at the pamphlet while she sipped her water. "What a splendid face! What is her full name?"

"Kata Dalström. Our Kata. The friend of the workers. There isn't a lockout where you won't find Kata encouraging the men when their own courage has given out."

My sister Elsa looked from Gärda's blazing eyes to the eyes of the woman on the pamphlet. "You resemble one another," she told Gärda, and Gärda grew red. Tears came to her eyes.

"That's such a great thing you just told me, Fröken Elsa. I feel my life hasn't been lived in vain. To look like the woman every working Swede respects means more to me than gold," she said, hurrying toward the kitchen door. "I shall be late at my post." And she flung herself out into the black night.

"Do you want a second glass of water," I asked Elsa. I was refilling my own at the tap. But Elsa didn't answer. She stood gazing at the pamphlet called "Shame!"

———

One evening there was blood on my nightgown.

Blood on my nightgown!

Elsa came into our bedroom. I hid the bloodstain with both my hands.

"Blood?" Elsa asked, matter-of-factly.

I blushed, I almost vomited from disgust. I looked toward the window, decided to throw myself out.

72

"Throw your nightgown in the laundry, not yourself out of the window," Elsa said. "I almost did the first time I menstruated. I'll bring you some sanitary towels."

"Sanitary towels?"

"Mormor knits them for her daughters, for her granddaughters. You will wear sanitary towels three days of the month. Then it's over—till next month."

Waves of nausea washed over me. I felt sick.

"Yes, it's repulsive," Elsa said. "It's repulsive to become a woman; it's repulsive to be a woman. We menstruate like bitches, stink like bitches, breed like bitches!"

"Now I'll leave you to yourself, Edit," Elsa said. "Leave you to think. You're going to go through another rough patch. You'll have to face a new situation. Life is a series of new situations to be faced. I told you that once before—remember. And with each new phase, one must change. I know, it's hell! Yet change and growth are synonymous."

I lay weeping in the dark. I hated the feel of the sanitary towel between my legs. My body was no longer a clean child's body. It did things without my permission. Bled when it felt like it, stunk when it felt like it. What a disgusting word, menstruation. How many millions of women were there on earth? Hundreds of millions? Our earth must be saturated with their awful menstruation blood. I wept.

———

That rough patch lasted two years. I was avoided, shunned; in self-defense I avoided, shunned everyone. In my class, I was the worst pupil in every

73

subject. Except in literature and history. In those two subjects, I was at the top.

The great historian, Fröken Lithner, had become our permanent history professor. But she ignored everyone except me, because of my classmates' lack of interest in her absorbing subject.

"Edit, I've infected you with my virus," she told me one day. She sounded delighted. "Your passion for history will last you all your life!"

Fröken Bratt said the same thing about literature: "I've given you my own heavenly illness! You'll be a voracious reader all your life. Here. Read these books by Selma Lagerlöf, the first Swedish woman to receive the Nobel Prize. The first woman ever to receive it. Read her, read all she ever wrote."

Twice a month, Fröken Bratt read my essays aloud to the class. She looked at me with a smile I didn't understand.

"You always read Edit's pieces. Not ours. It's unfair," a classmate complained.

"I read the best. Don't question my literary judgment," Fröken Bratt said dryly. "If your essays become better than Edit's, I'll read your essays, my girl."

Fröken Bratt was angry. "Edit observes. Why don't you? Why don't you girls bother to see things for yourselves, to think for yourselves, to use your imagination? Eh?" she asked. "Eh?"

But a blow was on the way because of my passion for reading, my passion for writing.

Greta delivered it: she loved to deliver blows.

"Edit has created another scandal, mor. She has written propaganda."

"Propaganda? But she's a child."

Mor sat playing her piano, exhausted by what Elsa called her non-life. "Tell me about it," she said, uninterestedly, to Greta.

"Tell all of us about it," said Maud.

"It's about some salt mines," Greta said in her doomsday voice. "Edit's class has been learning about mines, England's coal mines, Sweden's iron mines, Poland's salt mines, and so on. The girls were told to write essays on life in the mines."

"Life in the mines?" Maud laughed. "Who cares about life in the mines?"

"Edit chose to write about the salt mines of Poland," said Greta. "It seems they bring young ponies down into the mines to pull the salt carts. The ponies quickly grow blind in those dank, pitch-black lanes. Their bones, gums, muscles rot from the salt. They're never once in their lives brought up to the surface. They die fast. The same goes for the human salt workers."

"What's that got to do with Edit?" asked mor. One finger, which was as white and thin as a newborn asparagus, trailed across the keys of her piano.

"Edit suggested in her essay that the sons of the rich Polish mine owners should be lowered into their papa's mines—like their papa's tortured ponies. If the rich papas don't care about the suffering of defenseless young horses, then why should they bother about the sufferings of young men? They say that Edit is a socialist, mor."

"So-cia-list?" shuddered mor. "She's a child."

I looked up from Selma Lagerlöf's *Jerusalem*. "Socialist?" I asked.

"Oh, don't pretend you haven't heard of the socialists. Don't pretend you haven't heard of awful Branting," snapped Greta. "He and his gang, they're all socialists."

I looked at Greta whose face had gone red.

"Don't deny that you don't know about all the strikes," she cried.

All at once I, too, got angry. "Where do I ever get to know anything," I asked. "Not at home. Not at school. Home and school. I don't know any other worlds. How'd I get to know anything? How?" I cried.

But Greta shut me up.

"Well, you have to apologize in school for your stupid essay on the salt mines. Just say that you read all that nonsense in a silly newspaper."

"I didn't," I said. "I never see a newspaper. I learned about the mines in class. Besides, I do think the sons of the rich mine owners should be made to work the way their papas work the ponies and the miners. Should I say I don't think so? Mor, you taught us never to lie. Should I lie to save my skin? Should I lie, mor?"

Mor looked away from me, and I looked away from her. I felt ashamed for mor. Then I gave a start. For Elsa was looking straight into my eyes, and shaking her head.

"Jump!"

Three girls were lined up between me and the dreaded leather-horse, across whose high back we were forced to leap daily in our gym hall. As always

76

my heart flew into my mouth with fright. In a second
I'd be made to leap, swing myself onto the too-high
"horse" and jump into the void without faltering. And
without falling. We hated our cruel, headless horse.

"Edit!"

I sprang. I straddled the horse, then I flew into the
void. I all but died of fright.

"Beautiful," our gym teacher said. "Edit, I want
to speak to you after class."

"I've decided to make you second platoon
leader," Fröken Leander told me in her little office.
"You're not the tomboy type, afraid of nothing. You
are physically delicate. But you've managed to get
control of your nerves. You've got nerve—not nerves.
You'll take over the second ski platoon as well."

A platoon leader! It was the first responsible position I'd ever been given in school. It gave me more
pleasure than anything that had ever happened to me.

Every Saturday Fröken Leander took our class
skiing. Sometimes she led us to the high ski jump on
Ladugårds Gärde. The Saturday after my nomination
as platoon leader, she told me to take six girls to the
dreaded high jump and make them spring into the
snowy void. I knew how terrified they were. My voice
squeaked as I ordered: "Jump!"

The first girl and the second girl dived into the air
like fearless birds, the third girl jumped clumsily, the
fourth and the fifth giggled with fright, flung themselves off the platform, fell, shrieked, laughed. The
sixth one wouldn't jump.

"Jump, Bett!" I cried. I counted. "One, two,
three." But Bett threw herself down on the ski platform, and burst into tears.

Fröken Leander skied over to her.

"Edit, order Bett to jump."

77

I, too, skied over to Bett. I bent down.

"Are you terribly scared, Bett? We're all of us scared. But we must obey orders," I murmured in her ear.

"You're not to comfort Bett, platoon leader. Make Bett obey. To obey is one of life's fundamentals. Ski jumping makes youth courageous," roared fröken with the voice of an army sergeant. But I shook my head.

"Bett can't jump, fröken. She has worked herself into a state of hysterics. She'd break a leg if she jumped."

"You defy me, Edit Toll?"

"Fröken, Bett is as stiff as a frozen branch from fright. She might kill herself if I forced her to jump."

"You are dismissed, Edit. You're no longer my platoon leader," shouted fröken. She was beyond herself with fury. "What is your answer? Will you make Bett jump, or will you not? Yes or no?"

"No!"

My new happy world crashed about me. I was no longer platoon leader. Once more I'd become a nonentity.

"I'll never force anyone to do anything against their will," I said and was ordered to leave. I skied off. I was finished.

The next day Fröken Leander summoned me to her little office behind the gym hall.

"I'm about to be dismissed, Edit. I made Bett jump. She sprained her ankle. She has had a nervous breakdown. Her father claims it's my fault."

"It is his fault, fröken," I cried. "He made Bett a coward. We've known her since we were eight. We know she's a rotten coward. Poor Bett."

I wondered what our gym teacher would do if she

78

was kicked out. She told me. Speaking to herself more than to me, she said that her "god" was Professor Ling who, a hundred years ago, had made daily calisthenics obligatory in all of Sweden's schools.

"Professor Ling wanted to create a nation as fearless as the ancient Vikings," fröken said ecstatically. "He wanted Sweden's boys and girls to have Greek bodies." She looked at me: "Thanks to our iron-hard calisthenics, you've got a lithe, slim, supple body, Edit." Suddenly Fröken Leander asked me: "How old do you think I am, Edit?"

"Forty, fröken?"

"I shall soon be sixty," she said. "I shall have difficulty in finding another job if I'm dismissed. I shall be poor. Yet I don't regret having made Bett jump."

She got up.

"How do you think I'd look today if I hadn't been as hard on myself as I am with my girls? Well, I'll show you," Fröken Leander said and deliberately crumpled up. The steel-muscled athlete became an aged woman with a hunched back, a sagging neck; and her head hung forward like the head of any oldster. Her hands plucked at her gym tunic. Her expression became as aimless and dithery as—Bett's expression.

"This is the posture of a slack, self-indulgent, pampered and useless old female, fit for the rubbish heap."

She took an eager step toward me.

In a second she'd transformed herself into a young, straight, strong woman.

"Oh, *fröken!*"

She beamed. "I've shown you two women. It'll help you in your own life. One of the two women I portrayed will get a job. The other one won't. You needn't ask me which woman I've chosen to be. Remember my favorite word, Edit: to choose!"

———

The bigger we four sisters grew, the more our flat shrunk.

"I've just found a larger flat," cried mor one day. "Just two streets up. We'll still face Vallhallsvägen. I'll still be close to my beloved trees."

"Who'll pay the large rent?" asked Greta dryly.

"Your father. You must write him tonight. Tell him we need more money. Urgently." Mor's silk-voice changed as it always did when it said, "your father." But then her eyes got their new, special look, "Everything will turn out all right," she murmured. "Someone's looking after me."

"God, eh?" said Maud. She ran off, and the door slammed behind her. Elsa hurried after her, and we heard her scold Maud for having mocked mor. Greta joined them: their quarrel grew into a brawl.

"That's all your big sisters do nowadays, fight," wept mor. "When they were small they adored one another—adored me. They've become fiends." But mor cheered up: "Everything will be better in the big flat, Edit. We shan't be so much on top of one another."

It got worse. Far couldn't send more money: he didn't have any. So we couldn't pay the bigger rent. One day they cut the electricity.

"Give me the money that Morbror Victor gave you for your birthday," Greta told me.

"I'm saving it for a pair of skis, Greta."

"Give it," she ordered.

They cut off the gas.

"Maud. Give me the money that mormor sent you for Christmas," said Greta.

"I've spent it. Yesterday. On a new blouse," Maud said, and Greta told her to take the blouse back to the shop and ask them to refund her the money. Maud danced off. She returned with the new, smart blouse and a pair of scissors. She cut a hole in the hem of the blouse.

"*You* ask the shop to refund the money, Greta," she laughed. Her blue eyes were as hard as two marbles.

In our new flat whose rent we couldn't pay, everyone began disliking everyone else—from sheer anguish. How were we to survive? Everyone squabbled on the smallest pretext. Maud began to dislike Elsa for being more beautiful than herself, Greta disliked both of them because of her own plainness and lack of success at parties. Hanna grew still more deaf in her lonesome kitchen. Mor kept praying and weeping. She no longer touched her piano. I hid between the covers of books.

"We haven't a penny," sobbed mor. "What'll we do?"

"Sell," answered Greta.

"Sell what, Greta?"

"All our heirlooms. Farmor Horn's antiques. I'll phone the museum right away," Greta said, and the next day a mouse crept into our flat. He rubbed his paws.

"Have all these beautiful things come down to you from your husband's mother? From Countess Matilda Horn? From her ancestral estate, Åminne? Treasures, ah treasures," he squeaked. He looked about him ecstatically. He took out his pocketbook. "I'll pay for your collection of ancient silver right away. My men will fetch it all tomorrow." Again he looked about him. Then he gave an excited squeak.

"The escritoire," he cried. He twirled his mouse-whiskers. "Eighteenth-century French? Inlaid. A little jewel."

"No!"

Mor had placed herself before Farmor Horn's writing desk, protecting it with her out stretched arms.

"It is not for sale. My mother-in-law wrote all her letters on it. And her little diary. Please, I'm feeling indisposed. Dizzy . . ."

"I'll take my leave," squeaked mouse. "Have I tired you? I got carried away. Please accept my apologies. All this beauty. Genuine Swedish antiques. A treasure trove," he said once again, then bowed himself out. But as he tripped on a hole in our worn-out carpet, he smiled to himself.

"I feel that we'll meet soon again," he squeaked. "Very soon." He looked meaningfully at our poverty-stricken carpet. "Very, very soon," he said gleefully. "Au revoir."

When the door closed behind him, tears were seeping from mor's eyes. She stood rigidly still before her beloved writing desk.

———

Mor looked frozen. I ran over to her. I tore her hands off the desk, I pushed her down into her own sofa before the fire, I threw sad-coat over mor's stiff little body. I covered up all of mor, but her hand crept out and began to pluck at a wool-tuft the way we sisters did when we felt miserable. I crawled in beside mor. I took her in my arms.

"The museum will rob you girls of everything that belonged to your ancestors. Forever! Strangers will gaze at our treasures in the museum; strangers will touch them," said mor.

I squeezed her harder. I couldn't understand why some murky heirlooms had put her into such a frantic state.

"They won't get farmor's little writing desk," I promised her. "Elsa and I will lug it up into the garret. Tonight. We'll hide it behind farfar's big trunks. The museum man won't find it when he returns," I vowed.

Mor sat up so violently that sad-coat slipped to the floor.

"Will you? Oh, will you really? Yes, yes, stow it away behind your farfar's old leather trunks. Promise, Edit?"

"Will you dance with me if I save your writing desk, mor? Will you? You'll see that everything will be all right," I reassured her.

"Nothing has ever been all right for me, Edit. Everything was wrong from the beginning. Maud sneers at me because I love God. Greta sneers at me because I can't remember historical dates. Oh, I know I know nothing. Our governess taught us nothing. She knew nothing. She taught us a smattering of French, but all I remember is to ask permission to go to the toilet. *Permettez-moi d'aller au plaisir d'été.*"

I couldn't help laughing. "*Plaisir d'été!*"

"And before I was out of the nursery, my father married me to . . ."

"Far."

"I was sixteen and young for my age. Your far

came riding over to Sjögård one day, saw me playing with a doll on the lawn, fell in love with the girl with the doll, and asked for her hand. I wasn't even consulted. Ah, Edit, kill yourself rather than marry without love. It is terrible. As you're only a child, I can't explain the details of a loveless union. The horror of it," wept mor.

I kissed her hand that had been given away so wantonly to a nobleman she didn't like. Poor mor! Poor far! Suddenly something happened. Something big. Mor and I exchanged parts. I ceased to be her child; she became mine. I would protect mor forever and ever, I vowed to myself.

"I'll protect you, mor. Always! I'll work for you. I'll steal for you. I'll do murder for your sake," I said.

But mor didn't listen to me. She was lost in her bitter memories.

"It was a step up for my family to have a daughter married into the inaccessible Swedish aristocracy," she said. "My sisters married professional men, one married a judge, another one the mayor of the town of Örebro. Ordinary people? But I . . ."

"You, mor?"

"At seventeen I was sent to Stockholm to live with your far's mor in order to learn an aristocratic manner. Mind you, not just manners. A manner! There's a world of difference between those conceptions. I was taught how a lady enters a room, how she leaves it. How she sits down, how she gets up. I was taught that a noblewoman must at all times be . . . amiable. And unobtrusive. Gentle and dignified. I was told that one's movements show one's breeding. I was told that one's smile, one's laughter, the very expression of one's face divulge one's background to discerning eyes."

"Oh, mor!"

"Farmor Horn made me feel it was a matter of life and death that I acquire the grand manner before she introduced me to the Stockholm I would enter upon my marriage to her son," sighed mor.

"Why have you been teaching us a manner if you thought it was silly, mor?"

She sat up as straight as a lit candle.

"It isn't silly. Farmor Horn was right. A manner is all-important in our world. Rich women can buy fur coats. But a manner can't be bought. A manner takes one's entire childhood, one's entire youth to acquire. Thank heavens I've given you the manners of the world. How else would I find the right kind of husbands for four penniless daughters?"

"Husbands, mor? The right kind of husbands?" Again I burst into laughter. But mor wept.

———

"That weeping," sighed Elsa.

We'd just lugged mor's little writing desk up to the garret, and Elsa'd sat down on a broken chair. I was straddling Polle. Our childhood rocking horse had no eyes, and when I kicked his flanks to make him rock, he didn't budge. He'd stood so long in our damp garret his legs had grown rheumatic.

"Mor weeps because of losing some heirlooms," I said, looking at the inlaid writing desk that we had hidden behind some mildewy leather trunks. "Why does she care about heirlooms?" I laughed.

Elsa didn't laugh. Elsa had changed. She had stopped being close to giddy Maud; she joked less; she went to fewer parties. She thought. I'd find her

85

gazing out of a window for an hour; I'd see her lean against her bookcase—thinking. I wondered about Elsa. But she wasn't a person one could ask about herself.

"Speaking of mor, I once told you that life consists of a series of changes, Edit. Mor, however, couldn't change. She has remained a child, hence clings to childish things—like belongings, heirlooms like her inlaid writing desk, old silver—that kind of rubbish," said Elsa.

She looked at the moldy objects in the garret.

"Once this junk had a reason for existing. The trunks traveled. The chairs were sat on. But they've served their time. They're useless. Dead—like mor." Elsa drew her finger across the outmoded trunk on which she sat, and dust flew up. "Objects can't change," she said. "Human beings must."

She drew the word *mor* in the dust.

She remained silent. Silence had become a habit with her. I wanted her to go on talking to me. To clarify things for me. No one ever explained anything; and Elsa knew much, understood much.

"Elsa—" I began.

But she was lost in her own dreams.

"Let me explain metamorphosis to you," she said. "A young woman must change into a middle-aged woman. Then she must 'metamorphose' herself into an old woman of fifty—then sixty, then seventy. It demands courage. For it hurts to metamorphose oneself. Mor, like a child, can't bear to be hurt. So she weeps like a little child."

I patted Polle's mane: a moth flew out. Poor Polle. Poor mor.

"Poor mor," I said to Elsa, but she never let go of a subject before she'd exhausted it.

"Birds kick out their offspring when their baby-down has grown into tough feathers—capable of flight. Time is the parent-bird that throws all of us out of our various, cozy nests. Time forces us to grow wings strong enough to enable us to ride the storms of life."

"Our mor never grew adult feathers," cried Elsa. "She got stuck in an era when useless possessions meant something. Mor and her friends are anachronisms; our whole class is an anachronism. The very word class is an obsolete conception.

"Ugh, let's get out of here, Edit. I feel stifled among this dusty rubbish. Just as I've begun to feel stifled in our outmoded world. In our outmoded way of thinking, of living."

Elsa tore open the door to the musty garret. Young air slapped our faces. We drew deep breaths.

"Edit, never stop—metamorphosing yourself." Elsa closed the door to the garret behind us with a bang. It was as if she wanted to turn her back on the musty smells of the past forever. She raced down the stairs. "I'm going for a walk. I need fresh air!" she cried.

It was on the next night that Elsa died. It had been a dull, everyday evening. As always mor sat huddled before the fire; as always Greta had studied statistics; Maud had thrown a fit. Elsa had found hairs darker than her own on her beloved hairbrush, and she had hit Maud with the brush. Maud had howled with fury.

Suddenly Greta had had a fit, too. She'd announced she was leaving home for good, that she couldn't bear home any longer.

"I'm leaving Stockholm. I'll take up some position in the country," she'd declared and had marched out of the room. As always I had crept into my hiding place between the two covers of a book.

"Fasten my bracelet for me."

Elsa stood in the doorway of our room. Her pink ballgown fitted her body like an extra skin, her shining hair fitted her head like a cap of gold. But she was in a hurry. She was upset because of her fight with Maud, because of Greta's unusual outburst. Oh. If Elsa had asked me to admire her in all her glory, I'd not only have fastened her bracelet for her, I'd have kneeled before her, kneeled to her beauty.

"Fasten it yourself," I said grumpily. And I went to bed.

In the middle of the night, I heard my sister Greta speaking over the phone; I struck a match to look at the time. Who'd phone us at two o'clock in the morning?

"Yes?" Greta said into the phone, then, slow, very slow, "ye-es?"

Maud and I jumped out of our beds and ran to the dark little hallway where the telephone was. Mor, too, came hurrying in her long, white nightdress.

"Has something happened? To Elsa?" whispered mor.

Greta's eyes stared from their sockets. Her hand clenched the receiver so hard that her knuckles looked like pebbles.

"Is Elsa hurt, Greta?" whispered mor.

"Yes, mor."

"Is Elsa . . . dead, Greta?" whispered mor.

"Yes, mor!"

All that night we sat on mor's bed. She didn't move. None of us moved. None of us spoke. We held hands. Dawn came but we still didn't move; we still didn't speak. At eight o'clock heavy steps stomped up our stairs.

"They're bringing her home," Greta whispered.

"Bringing who home?" I whispered back.

"Our Elsa."

"Elsa!"

The awful steps stopped in our drawing room. Then all was silent. Greta's quiet voice told me to get dressed. "Run down and get Elsa some flowers, Edit dear."

I bought a bouquet of daffodils. They were so crazy with spring they jumped into my arms, wanting to get out into my arms, wanting to get out into the sunshine. The sun blazed. Some sparrows pecked about in some horse shit: the day was wild with happiness. I brought home my bouquet, opened the window, and flung it into our dirty courtyard. I didn't want my ecstatic flowers to touch the . . . the thing that lay in our drawing room.

"Bring Elsa her flowers," Greta whispered to me through the half-open door.

"I just threw them out of the window," I said.

"Oh, Edit! At least come in and say goodbye to our . . ." Greta's voice broke, "our Elsa."

Elsa lay in her pink ballgown on mor's sofa. Her long hair covered the gash in her neck where the jugular vein had been severed. She had stepped out on the glass floor of a winter garden where the ball had been held. It was covered with grass, and she had thought it was a solid floor. Elsa had crashed through the glass, had cut her jugular vein, had died instantly, they'd told Greta over the phone.

I stood looking at Elsa.

Mor, Greta, Maud stood weeping by the sofa.

I didn't weep. I thought. I thought that one goes to a party in a pink ball dress—alive. One comes home in a pink ball dress—dead.

All at once I felt happy! I had understood something! One minute one was alive; the next minute one was dead. I felt elated at the thought of the minutes, the hours, the years that lay ahead of me. I'd never waste one! Not—one—single—minute. Oh! Suddenly I realized that I knew more about life than mor, more than Greta, than Maud: I knew more than anyone!

I ran down to our courtyard, snatched Elsa's daffodils from the dirty snowdrifts, dashed upstairs, lay the bouquet on the swatch of blond hair that hid my sister's wound.

My Elsa's wound.

Elsa!

———

"Christ gave his life for man," said Pastor Björk, who confirmed me that spring.

"A feat."

"What did you say, Edit? I thought I heard you make a remark," said the pastor.

"I've read that Christ never existed, Pastor Björk. I heard he was invented by the four apostles!"

Pastor Björk raised his eyes to heaven.

"That kind of book ought to be burned. Cast into

the devouring flames," he cried passionately. But he didn't look angry. He had officiated at my sister's funeral only last week.

"The great day is approaching," he told our group. "Your confirmation day. Dear young girls, you will partake of the flesh of the Son of God. You will drink His Holy Blood. Prepare yourself for the big moment. Get into a state of grace. Let's pray."

I looked at the pastor. He had a very stubborn face. While the others prayed, I thought of the book Elsa had lent me, that he wanted burned. The book said that once upon a time savages had fashioned littled stone gods because they were frightened of thunder, of wild animals, of their fellow savages and because they hoped their stone gods would protect them. According to Elsa's book, our god was also an invention. Exploiters of human labor had invented a god their slaves would fear, a vengeful deity that kept their slaves docile. I didn't pray. I sat picking off some dry skin on my thumb.

We'd scraped together enough money for an ugly white confirmation dress, and on the big day I kneeled, feeling I looked hideous, before the altar in the company of a dozen tearful girls. My own eyes were dry. I'd arrived at a conclusion. In order to carry it out, I kept repeating sentences from that book that Pastor Björk had objected to.

"To eat the flesh of Christ is to return to cannibalism," the book said. It said, too, that we Swedes used to sacrifice horses at our midwinter festivals, and drink their steaming blood. The Swedes thought it made them strong. But little by little, the barbaric custom had stopped. "It is high time," Elsa's book said, "that another pagan practice, the drinking of the blood of a fictitious 'Christ,' stops, too."

Pastor Björk gave the girl next to me a wafer to eat: if I didn't act quickly he'd make me eat a wafer too. Pastor Björk would turn me into a cannibal.

The wafer lay on my tongue; Pastor Björk mumbled some words and moved on to the next weeping girl. Quickly I lifted my embroidered handkerchief and spat out Pastor Björk's Christ. And now I was ready to carry out the second part of my vow. Only just in time. The pastor was pouring red wine into the gullets of all the girls. I coughed, pretending to choke: thus I got rid of Christ's "blood." It seeped into the little handkerchief that mor had embroidered for the occasion.

For the first time in my depressed puberty-years, I felt strong. Free! So moral actions weren't harder than physical actions, such as high ski-jumping. I felt happy. I wanted to sing a gay polka tune. I wanted to laugh. I choked it down. Pastor Björk gave me a long, long look.

It was over; I dashed home. I jumped over a pile of stones; I jumped over a small hillock of snow, giddy with joy. For I knew that I had just taken a high, moral ski jump.

"Are you able to eat a little something?" mor asked me softly. "Some girls are so moved after their First Communion they are unable to swallow a thing, dear. One's confirmation is such a tremendous experience, isn't it," cried mor ecstatically. "Child, Hanna has prepared a little treat for you. But if you feel that you can't eat . . ."

I wolfed down steak and onions.

———

"We'll fetch Elsa's ashes today," Greta said.

"We?"

Yes, you and me. Mor is too ill to come. Maud, too."

Mor hadn't left her room since Elsa's death, nor Maud ours. Maud had broken out in a nervous skin rash. She kept raving about Elsa's hairbrush.

"Elsa loved her clean hairbrush. She loved her hair," sobbed Maud. "She wanted her hair to shine, so she washed her brush every day. To annoy her I used it, leaving it full of my hair. I did it all the time. Elsa hated it. Now I can never beg her forgiveness. I'll never meet her again. Or is there a life after this, do you think, Edit?"

"No," I said.

Greta begged me: "Do come with me to the cemetery, Edit. Mor wants Elsa to be buried in the countryside. We'll ship her ashes by rail."

We took the tram to Haga Cemetery.

"This way, lady."

The guard's voice sounded as matter of fact as if he were a grocer about to show us his wares. In the downstairs room where he brought us, he pointed to a shelf lined with labeled containers.

"Toll, eh?" he asked Greta. "Here's her can."

(Can?)

"I'll wait outside," I whispered to Greta.

"No, please," she whispered.

I went over to the window. It was spring, therefore horrid. The day was icy and black. I stood staring at the horrid spring day.

I heard Greta give a gasp. I turned round.

The man had shoved his hand into Elsa's "can," and his great fingers came up holding a little handful of pale, silken ashes, a few tiny bones. Was this Elsa?

93

Was this death? Oh! A week ago Elsa had done something that people called "dying"! I'd seen her a few hours after she'd done it. Today I saw my sister Elsa as a fistfull of ashes. Death was simple. People had lied to me about death. They had told me it was holy. They'd told me it was awe-inspiring. It was nothing of the kind. Death was just a few ashes of the same kind the peasants in Sjögård spread on the fields to make things grow. Bone meal. I began to sing behind my face. I felt happy. Happy!

Greta and I took the tram back to Stockholm. Greta and I brought the bone meal back to Stockholm.

———

Once, in Sjögård, I'd sown some parsley grains, but they didn't sprout. "Why don't they come up?" I'd asked Holger. "It's not the moment," he said. "There's a moment for them to come up."

Now I ran to mor's drawing room.

"My pimples! Where have they gone to?"

"I told you they'd disappear. There's a moment for everything. A moment for pimples to appear, a moment for pimples to disappear."

She scanned my face. "Your skin is as clear as a lake, Edit. It's as fair as the sky in summer."

A few months later in the sauna baths I shouted to Maud: "They've come! My breasts, Maud."

"Why not? It's the moment for them to come," Maud said as matter-of-factly as Holger. "There's a moment for things to happen. There are moments for things not to happen," she said as quietly as mor. "Did you expect your tits never to show up?"

We stood, naked, in the hot room of our sauna bath. Maud gave my body a scrutinizing look.

"You'll have big and high breasts when they get ripe. Because of their size, your body'll be better than mine."

"Yours is beautiful."

"But yours will be perfect. Your hips are long. Your legs are long. And your hair is—endlessly long. Oh, you have a line, Edit. A line. That's the most important thing."

I laughed with happiness. I smiled at Maud.

"Your smile is the best thing about you. It's returned. I mean, the smile you had when you were a child. When you were a little girl. It is irresistible," Maud said. "Irre-sis-ti-ble!"

"Oh, Maud!"

"For years you've been an ugly toad," she laughed. "Overnight you have changed. You'll become a charmbag once more."

That night I wept myself to sleep. From joy! In the middle of the night, I woke up, remembering that something extraordinarily nice had happened to me, something tremendous that would change my life. But I must be wrong. Nothing had ever come my way. I jumped out of bed; I let my nightgown drop; I stood naked before our long mirror. And the moon shone on my naked body.

I knelt.

I knelt to myself in the moonlight . . .

———

We couldn't afford to buy new clothes, clothes that would fit my fast-growing limbs. Another piece of luck. My bosoms, gathering volume like snowballs, pushed out the cloth of my aged, too-tight coat; my short, worn-out skirt showed my slim legs.

"Hi! You there!" A street boy shouted to me in the park; and for the first time in my life, I didn't hang my head in shame and toadlike embarrassment. I smiled at him. He smiled back. I began to run. I jumped across a snowdrift for joy. I took some dance steps. I was on my way to Farbror Karl's yearly family party.

"Dance, Edit?"

"Me?"

No one had ever asked me to dance at family parties. Now everyone asked me. I danced with Cousin Karl twice; Cousin Axel cut in.

"I'm her cousin too. It's my turn."

"You have a face like a white apple," Cousin Axel said. "Have you ever been kissed?"

"Kissed? Me?"

"I like to kiss everything that's round," Cousin Axel said. We danced. Oh, how we danced.

"Remember the white Astrakhan apples in Sjögård, Edit?" Axel asked. "Early in the morning there used to be dew on them. One morning I picked up an Astrakhan apple and kissed it."

"Kissed—an apple?"

"I'm going to kiss you!" Axel kissed me. "Let's dance together the whole evening," he murmured in my hair.

I went from embrace to embrace that night, just the way I'd done when I was small, just the way I'd done when everyone, aunts and uncles, wanted to kiss my round face. That night, at Farbror Karl's family party, everyone seemed pleased that I had recovered from the terrible illness of puberty.

"Charmbag," laughed Maud.

She was dancing by me. "Edit, I'm sneaking off. Family parties bore me. Coming home, too?"

Home? I'd forgotten I had a home. I was too wildly happy. Did mor's corner by the fire still exist? Did mor exist? All at once I decided I'd never go home again.

"I'm not coming home," I called out to Maud. "I'm not coming home, Maud," I cried out to her. Never going home, never going home again . . .

———

That Sunday I should have been studying. Our final examinations loomed, and I should have been writing the speech that each of the out-going girls had to give before a body of teachers. Much depended on one's speech: it was supposed to show maturity.

I'd forgotten all about it. I'd plunged myself into the reading of Selma Lagerlöf's *The Saga of Gösta Berling*, and I ate her words. I wondered what her secret was. Her sentences jumped from the pages into one's dazzled eyes. Her miraculous writing had made the old men of the Swedish Academy give the Nobel Prize to a desiccated, homely, lame spinster.

Selma Lagerlöf never decked out a sentence. She never put a frill on it. Her simplicity made me tremble with joy. She never insisted; she never kept on at one. And she didn't show off cleverness. She didn't even seem clever. But she was full of talent as a dog's hide is full of fleas.

What was talent?

I began to sing. I still had no voice, but there was

no one at home. Maud was out amusing herself; mor was sitting in church staring at Christ. Deaf Hanna dozed in her kitchen in our new, very small flat. So I sang at the top of my lungs. Then I stopped singing. I read. I read magic Selma Lagerlöf's magic words. I started to sing again, louder this time.

Suddenly I grabbed a pencil and began to write about homely old Selma. Because she had been lame, children hadn't wanted to play with her: she'd spent her childhood listening to the sagas of Sweden's kindly tomtar, Sweden's wicked trolls, told her by her grandmother. In their wilderness home amidst snow and ice, the old lady had told Selma about Sweden's Norsemen who, still in the twentieth century, had Viking blood coursing through their wild veins.

Selma Lagerlöf said that Swedes could never be tamed. They'd become "Christianized" a thousand years later than the rest of the world. Besides, our Norsemen paid no heed to the foreign Christian priests who, in their long, effeminate skirts, invaded the Scandinavian wildernesses. Like buzzing black flies, they baptized the Norsemen, with the Bible in one hand while the other hand held a murderous axe. Soon, however, the Norsemen kicked out the sniveling priests from their storm-whipped shores.

I read; I read. I began to write. I sang. Then read. Then wrote again.

I took out another book of old Selma's. This one was about love. Love, she wrote, burned one like hellfire. It made one's heart jump like a stag, like a doe, like a mad goat. That novel was called *The Saga of Gösta Berling* and had been translated into every language in the world.

I threw the novel to the floor, grabbed my pencil once more and started writing my speech. It would be about Selma Lagerlöf. I would analyze our magnificent Swedish language—the language to which she had given back its thrilling purity and simplicity of structure. I wrote about her use of hopping, dancing words, and of words that hid themselves like little children, in corners, and wept.

"What have you been doing with your lonely self all Sunday?" asked mor, returning from evensong, hymnbook in hand.

"Oh! Nothing of importance, mor."

———

To vomit was the solution. I had to escape from the torture chamber that was our classroom on speech day. I'd feign a stomach upset.

Agnes had spoken. On Bismarck, her hero. Ella, the mathematician of our class, had given her speech, telling about the discovery of mathematics by the Egyptians. They were knowledgeable, Agnes, Ella. They'd received applause and, realizing that they'd passed their ordeal, settled, smilingly, down at their desks.

"Edit Toll!"

I knew I was no longer physically repulsive, else I couldn't have crossed the floor that was ringed about with bespectacled, glaring teachers. The floor seemed as vast as the Sahara. I dragged myself across it, mounted the podium, sank down in our teacher's chair.

"Selma Lagerlöf and Her Writing," I said. No sound came out.

"*Louder!*"

A smile like a newborn infant had jumped from me the second I said the beloved name. Quickly, eagerly I began to speak about Sweden's greatest writer, telling about the golden bees that, daily, flew out from the hive that was her brain in order to gather the honey that Selma needed for her creative work. The honey was the images that author filled her extraordinary novels with. I ended the first part of my speech by saying that Selma Lagerlöf had invented a new Swedish. Her Swedish: our greatest cultural heritage.

Then I told them about Selma the woman. I spoke about her capacity for getting under the skin of the men and women who lived in her poverty-stricken parts of Sweden: about her skill in speaking with their voices, her skill in weeping their tears, laughing their laughter. No other writer in Sweden had known how to laugh Swedish laughter, which was different from all laughter in the world. "Not boorish and boisterous," I said. "Swedish laughter is quiet and serene."

"Go on, Edit!"

The principal's voice was so kind that the last blob of terror-vomit left my dry mouth. Besides, I no longer cared. I didn't care what anyone thought of my speech. I was talking about a giant, about a writer who belonged to me as much as to the erudite teachers who filled our classroom. I said, ecstatically, that Selma Lagerlöf hadn't received the Nobel Prize because of the literary brilliance she shared with dozens of Swedish writers, but because of her capacity for great, human love.

"To love like Selma Lagerlöf is genius! Great love and genius are synonymous!"

I got up. I had finished. I had said my say—and,

shit, if they flunked me, well those fuck-asses could all go to hell.

The applause was deafening.

"I've listened to our pupils' speeches for decades," the principal told me. "Your talk was inspired. Inspired by a great love for a great writer. It will be included in our school archives." She put her old hand on my shoulder. "Thank you for an unforgettable hour!"

I dropped her a deep curtsy. And then my hand was pressed by the bony old fingers of the other teachers. How plain the poor women were. No hand, I thought, had ever clasped theirs except Selma Lagerlöf's that clasped all hands who needed hers . . .

"Edit," one of the teachers said. She said no more, but I felt that my name had come to mean something to her. For once, not my last name. Not Toll. "Edit——" she repeated, gently.

———

Mor, always in despair, said, "I've heard that your final marks are shockingly bad. The chances are that you are not going to receive your university entrance certificate. You have failed in *too* many subjects, Edit."

I yawned. "We can't afford to send me to university in any case," I answered. "We're poor."

"You should have studied. You've spent ten years in Brummerska School. What have you learned?" asked mor, and I burst out laughing. "Not a fuck!" I said and mor shuddered.

"If you don't receive your certificate, you won't get a government job, which is the only kind of work a girl of your class can accept. Ah, child . . ."

———

I had other preoccupations. A dance circle had been formed in Stockholm with cadets from Sweden's nobility. Agnes Weidenhielm, Elsa Rosenblad, had already been invited to join it. Would I be asked to join that charmed circle? What was a school certificate compared to dancing with men?

"Telephone, mor!"

"I'm delighted, Countess von Platen," I heard mor say over the phone. "Edit, too, will be delighted. What is the name of the young man?" asked mor happily.

I had never heard her voice so gay.

"Child. Edit, you have been invited to join an exclusive dance circle, the most select group of young men and women in Sweden," mor told me. "All the members have ancient, historical names." She laughed with delight.

"In your dance circle, there is only one commoner. But his mother is titled. Countess von Platen asked if I minded.

"I said no," smiled mor. "In absurd England, people can buy titles, and rich manufacturers do," she said scornfully. "In France, the upstart Napoleon conferred titles on people we wouldn't receive in our kitchens! Only in Sweden is the nobility authentic, Edit."

Mor quickly made me a dance frock.

"How do I look?" I asked her on the evening of the big event, my first ball. I was nervous. "How shall I behave, mor?"

"Be yourself," mor said. "You're a lady born and bred. You had a perfect nursery education. You have spent ten years of your life in the strictest of all upper-class schools in the whole world."

For a moment she looked contented. Her worry frown, however, quickly came back.

"If only you had received your certificate, all would have been lovely," she sighed.

"What certificate, mor?"

"You have already forgotten. Your university entrance examination, of course. Ah, Edit, you live in a world of your own. What'll become of you in life?"

———

Chandeliers glittered on the gold-braided uniforms of ten ramrod-straight cadets; chandeliers shone on ten lithe, smiling girls. In the middle of the great drawing room, Count and Countess von Platen received: the aim of our dance circle was to prepare us for our future existences. We had been taught how to behave since we were in diapers. Now we were to be taught the easy elegance, the authority of those who ruled the world. We were to be initiated into a *monde* that would mark us, as Elsa once said, like branded cattle.

I watched, amazed, as Count von Platen scrutinized each light kiss the cadets placed on his wife's white-gloved hand: the monocle in his eye gleamed approvingly when a cadet performed the ritual to his satisfaction. His countess, too, seemed to feel it was a matter of life and death that her girls executed their curtsies with easy grace and modest charm.

The music started: my knees gave way. With my male cousins it had been easy: I'd gone from embrace to embrace. But here! With strangers!

But that night, too, I went from embrace to embrace. I danced all evening. I laughed all evening. Ever fresh cadets bowed before me:

"May I have this dance, Fröken Toll?"

"May I have this dance, Fröken Toll?"

"May I have this dance, Fröken Toll?"

I slid into new arms, ever new arms. I looked into eyes that smiled and glittered—and took my measure. Cadet Evers, the only commoner in the brilliant gathering was the handsomest of all. He was tall; he was slender in his pale blue uniform. We danced again, again. I laughed with joy each time he bowed before me.

"I've never met anyone as gay as you. Do you always laugh?" he laughed.

He held me very close, and all at once something happened to my body that had never happened to my body before: it grew limp. The harder he held me, the limper it became. I didn't dare look at him. When I finally dared, he had stopped smiling. He looked straight into my eyes: he held me tighter.

When I returned at midnight, mor was sitting up in her bed as straight as a lit candle.

"The minute you left, the phone rang, Edit. It was the principal herself. Fancy. The principal of your school herself. Child, your speech on Selma Lagerlöf swung the pendulum. It seems they thought it extraordinarily moving. You've got your certificate—although you've failed in other subjects. They say you're ripe for your certificate. A whole new future has opened up for you, Edit."

I smiled vaguely at mor. A whole new future had indeed opened up for me. Not only the one she visualized.

I'd meant to kiss her little nose good-night. I forgot all about it. I no longer saw mor's face. Where it had been all my life, other faces shone now, beckoned: the face of Folke, the eager face of Axel, the faces of Staffan, Gustaf.

I ran naked to the mirror. It was seven o'clock; no need to dress. I just wanted to make sure that my two great fruits still hung on the branch that was my body—and oh, they did. Hadn't they swelled in the last hour? They hurt. They always hurt before a ball: at the thought of men, my bosoms ripened like melons in sunlight.

Was that the church bells ringing? Eight chimes! I jumped into my balldress that was frayed from the long winter season, I slid my feet into slippers: they too were worn from too much waltzing. Now I had to dash out into the arctic Stockholm night.

"Let's dance, Edit. I'm in a state. I'm bursting," Folke whispered when I flitted into the ballroom. I, too, felt like a soap bubble about to burst.

"Oh, Folke!"

He danced me away from the crowd in the Cadet Institute's brightly lit ballroom; he steered me toward a half-open door. Swift as an eel his tongue slid into my mouth.

"You do care for me, Edit?" he whispered.

No, I didn't care for him. If I should care for every cadet who had wanted me to during the long, wild winter season, I'd be dead. From exhaustion. I didn't care for the cadets; I only cared about my ache. Wasn't that enough? Didn't the boys with whom I danced know about my ache? They did know. That's why they crowded about me, crushing my mouth with kisses.

Oh! Folke's tongue played like a fish in the wet lake of my mouth. Suddenly I got wet elsewhere. What did it mean? I had just had my monthly; it couldn't be my monthly. Then what was happening to my downstairs body? Oh, I never knew the answer to anything. I felt sure that my friends knew nothing about their bodies, either. Nice girls didn't. Servant girls knew everything. I envied them. But one thing I did know. I knew that men were my life. That nothing else mattered to me.

"Fröken Toll! Enjoying our ball?"

Folke and I flew apart; we were horrified at the sudden appearance of Captain von Uggle who was smiling at me. Folke glared at him with such spitting jealousy, the captain stuttered off.

"He's at least thirty. More! Maybe thirty-five. A dirty old man," Folke growled. "Let's dance, Edit. I'm in a state."

Again I was in Folke's arms. Again I began to ache. If only someone would explain to me why my body ached.

"You must begin to work, Edit!"

"No, mor."

I refused to sit cooped up in a government office like Greta, writing meaningless words on meaningless slips of paper.

"I'm always invited out, mor. I cost you nothing in food," I said. "And my little room isn't even heated. I've never cost anyone anything." All of a sudden I felt bitter.

Greta marched in with her government-office face. When she saw me dressed in my dance frock, she said, "Mor, do forbid Edit to go out tonight. The life she leads! Forbid her to accept every invitation she gets." She looked angrily at the row of engraved invitations that adorned our mantelpiece. "All for Edit! Mor, you must tell her to . . ."

"Leave Edit alone," said mor, gazing into the fire.

I gave a start. Mor was defending me? During the whole whirling winter season I'd barely noticed her, but now I felt grateful to her. I saw, surprised, that she still had her pretty little nose, and that her hands, her snow-white gloves, were still pressed to her worried cheeks. But swiftly Folke's face took the place that mor's face had occupied for the fraction of a second. Folke's face and the faces of Axel, of Stig, of Staffan— oh, of all of them.

"Edit looks like a sleepwalker," Greta said. "How I'd like to rub out that expression of hers. It comes from too much dancing. Ugh, her face looks . . ."

"Much will be written on Edit's face one day," mor said in her quiet voice. "Remember her teacher of literature wanted her to write," she said, but Greta said writing wasn't work.

"Edit must take a job," she snapped. "After all, Farbror Karl has found work for her at the Military

Institute. It won't remain vacant forever."

"Fuck-ass," I told her behind my face. "Shit-fart."
But mor was speaking to me.

"The pastor who confirmed you phoned while
you were out, Edit. Pastor Björk wants you to attend a
little gathering in his office. He explained what it was
about." I patted away a yawn. "Pastor Björk feels that
Stockholm's society girls are too busy amusing themselves to the exclusion of all else. He'd like the girls he
confirmed years ago to engage in good works. He
wants to enlist them in the service of our Lord."

"Our Lord?"

I wanted to laugh, but mor had stood up for me
against Greta, and I wanted to please her.

"I'll go to Pastor Björk's little party for our Lord. I
promise you I'll be there. Oh, mor, I must be off. I'm
due at a ball at nine."

———

"One—four—nine—eleven!"

Pastor Björk counted the votes that we'd thrown
into a silver cup that served as voting urn. His party
for the Lord had been a success: many girls he'd confirmed had turned up. Now all that remained for him
to do was to choose two of us to be his helpers. He
looked pleased with himself. He probably felt it had
been a good idea to select his helpmeets by voting.
"It's the fair way," he seemed to be saying to himself.
Oh, he was pleased with Pastor Björk!

"The two girls who get most votes will be my dear
helpers," he told his flock of dance-mad beauties.
We all knew he wanted Madeleine Carleson for

helpmeet—she was so dignified—and dumpy Elsa Rosenblad. They were *good* girls.

"I'll vote for you, Agnes," I whispered.

"And I for you," Agnes smiled, and I told my oldest friend that hers would be the only vote I'd get.

"Anyhow, who'd want to be one of Pastor Björk's ghastly helpmeets?" I laughed. "Even if I got votes, musty Björk wouldn't accept me. I never paid attention when he prepared us for our confirmation."

"Edit Toll. Edit Toll."

Pastor Björk scowled. I grinned. I'd received two votes. Who'd have believed it? Pastor Björk looked thunderous. Had he noticed, years ago, that I'd refused to eat Christ's flesh, had refused to drink Christ's blood when he failed to make me into a Christian? But perhaps the old hawk had noticed something quite different? Had his cold, canny eyes seen a thousand male kisses on my bruised lips?

"Edit Toll!"

The room giggled. My friends bit their lips. They looked from me to the fuming pastor; they couldn't help tittering. Some of them had been my schoolmates; perhaps they remembered my naughty drawings? Did they recall my wild stories? Perhaps they just liked me for being as dance mad as themselves!

"You're liked," Agnes whispered to me. She threw a look about Pastor Björk's musty office. "Our friends like you because you don't give a fig whether they do or don't. People who want to be liked are loathed. You don't make up to anyone."

"Sch-ss, girls!"

"Madeleine Carleson," cried Pastor Björk. He seemed to grow fatter. He took another vote from the silver cup. "Madeleine Carleson," he cried and grew still fatter from satisfaction. "Elsa Rosenblad! Elsa

Rosenblad!" he beamed, reading more votes. Things were looking up for the pastor. Perhaps he'd get the two helpers he wanted, god-fearing, steady girls. "It's getting late, dear friends. We must hurry," he said. He sounded jubilant. There were only a few votes left.

"Edit Toll, Edit Toll, Edit Toll."

But the next votes went to Madeleine Carleson. At the end, however, I'd received the majority. I wanted to laugh. Pastor Björk looked at Madeleine Carleson and made a little speech.

"I am happy our little group will be in your capable hands, Madeleine," he said. But then he remembered that the votes called for two helpers, and he turned reluctantly to me. "I'll be glad of your help, too, Edit," he said, ice in his smile. Quickly, he turned back to Madeleine.

"You will act as go-between, dear Madeleine. You'll find out what kind of good works each girl will want to do, then inform me. Ah, there is so much to be done in our unfortunate Stockholm. Such quantities of poor. Such quantities of uncared-for sick. Of course, one mustn't cavil against our Lord's plans. There will always be rich and poor: it's his will! Stockholm also has lots of cripples, lots of blind, deaf, and the neglected children of our drunken and shiftless factory workers. Lot of work for all of you. You see, life isn't all dancing, not all selfish enjoyment," said Pastor Björk. At that moment our eyes met.

"That's where you're wrong," my eyes told him. Dancing, kisses, men are everything. "At least to me, Pastor Björk. At least to me."

My legs were pulling at me. They couldn't sit still another minute. I sprang to my feet, aching to get away from the dim office where photographs of bishops hung on the walls like musty bats. The other girls too crowded toward the exit. But in the doorway, I turned my head as if something or someone had commanded me, and I looked straight into a face that held so much much pain I gasped. I ran back to Madeleine Carleson.

"Congratulations, Madeleine," I said, "for getting so many votes." But it was a look of defeat, not of victory, that stared at me from her frustrated eyes. I sucked in my breath. Oh! No male arms would be waiting for Madeleine tonight, nor on any other night. The horror of it. The horror of not being desired. Of nights without kisses.

"Congratulations," I said again. I felt a sob in my throat. But then I flung myself out into Stockholm, my Stockholm. The town of a thousand lights, of a thousand arms.

———

Well, here was Grefturegatan. And there was the crèche where I'd chosen to do my voluntary work.

"I like children," I'd told Madeleine, when we placed Pastor Björk's "girls" in various branches of "good works." "I like children, Madeleine!"

"Has fröken brought an overall?" the sister at the crèche asked me. Her voice was so meek it sounded like a sheep's bleating. "Our children are very dirty."

Dirty? An understatement, I thought. In the dim room crawled creatures who looked like clods of filth in motion, hideous gnomes who hit each other with blocks of wood. They stunk of the sewers from where they came. But I liked them. They looked just like the children of Sjögård, like the starvelings who were my first playmates, my first friends.

"What part of Stockholm do they come from, sister?"

"From the hidden slums round here. Their mothers are mostly factory workers, unmarried sluts nearly all of them," she said. But although the sister was as pious as Pastor Björk himself, she didn't seem shocked at the lack of wedding rings on her women's work-scarred hands. She, not the pastor, spent her days among the wretched and the sick, among the starving and the frightened.

"Will fröken begin by washing them? I haven't had time, for weeks. At home they never wash. There's no water in the garrets of the poor. There's a pump in the yards, but it's frozen solid half the year. Oh, dear, they do stink!"

I began to pull the rags off a boy called Gösta. Under his grime, he was as beautiful as a flower. He stood naked before me, and for the first time I saw a live penis. Good heavens! I remembered that Holger had one, too. But was that all there was to a penis, I thought. That little thing? Then why was it always hidden behind a fig leaf on male statues? Suddenly I remembered something else. Holger had told me that his organ would grow to the size of mormor's bull's when he grew up.

All at once a hidden-away memory jumped up from a hole in my mind, a picture of mormor's snorting bull pushing his male thing in and out of a young, golden cow. I blushed. That's why they glued fig leaves over men's organs: they became as enormous as that of mormor's Hercules! Would I, one day, have such as object pushed in, pulled out of my body? My breasts began to swell; my loins began to ache; I trembled with fear and longing. I lifted Gösta out of the tin tub and told him to dry himself on the communal rag.

Then I plunged a girl into the dirty tub. She'd never been in contact with water before and screamed.

"Sister, what shall I dress them in, now that they are clean? They smell good. They look like flowers," I said.

"That's the only clothing they own. They're children of workers, fröken," she said, and at that moment a new ache grabbed hold of me. Where was it seated, my new pain? In my head? No, it ran through my entire system. Was it caused by sister saying "children of workers" in her bleating, indifferent voice? It was the same voice that Moster Anna had used when she forbade me to play with the "brats of mormor's farmhands."

Workers, farmhands? Did everyone hate them? No one ever mentioned them in my world: nor their children, nor their hunger. Poverty was an unmentionable word in my family. Nor did my friends, nor did my dance partners ever speak of the black misery of those hundreds of thousands of Swedes who were forced to emigrate to America.

Were there two Swedens, two Stockholms? One as black as soot, the other as bright as lit chandeliers, I wondered as I poured the filthy bath water into the sink. My signet ring with my crest and crown slipped off. As I looked at it gleaming in the water something happened to me. What? I stared at the crest, the crown. My crest? My crown! I jumped when sister asked me to work faster. Feeling guilty, I picked the ring from the filthy water and put it back on my finger.

"It's late! The horde'll be arriving. The factory whistles have sounded. Here they come."

Clomp! Creatures with boots that looked like parodies of footwear, with long, dragging skirts whose hems dripped with melting snow, came scowling into the crèche, grabbed a screaming offspring, and set off into Stockholm's arctic night. I stood looking after them. It was the first time I had met factory hands. They looked like the peasant women of my childhood, only more worn, more ill. But one girl was different from the others. Her hair was frizzed, her lips were painted. She threw sister a mocking glance from under her blackened lashes, then she grabbed beautiful Gösta and danced off with him.

"Who is she, sister?"

"A streetwalker," sneered sister. "One day God will strike her dead on her beat."

"Her beat?"

"The street where she collects her customers. Her men. That's how she makes a living."

I stared at the bleating sheep. "I thought her lovely, as lovely as her little boy, as Gösta," I said. I stood thinking of the streetwalker's light walk, of the laughter that spurted from her lips, of her dyed ringlets, and I wondered if loving many men made a woman—lovely. I tore off my grubby overalls; I flung them on the bench. I put on my coat.

(The beat?)

———

"You're to be presented at court," mor said ecstatically.

"Shit!"

"Edit!"

"Forgive me. Oh, mor, forgive me." My childhood lay far behind me, and although Holger and his family had emigrated to America, Holger's vocabulary hadn't. It remained inside me, engraved on my brain.

"Must I be presented?" I asked.

"Of course you must. You're coming out this year," said mor. "The daughters of Sweden's nobility must be introduced to their queen. The custom has existed for centuries. It is from their midst the young officers of our crack regiments choose their spouses."

Laughter bubbled up inside me. I felt like a champagne bottle. I choked down the bubbles. I didn't want to hurt mor. I didn't want her nose to turn paler than it already was; I didn't want her hands to start torturing each other.

"It has an added advantage," mor prattled on. "The girls who are presented to Her Majesty are invited to all the receptions given by the diplomatic corps. That way they find husbands among the foreign attachés, the foreign secretaries. It is not for nothing that three foreign languages are obligatory in top schools like yours."

"What'll I wear at court? My balldress is in tatters," I laughed, and now mor's little nose did turn white.

"What's wrong with you, Edit? Why don't you ever know anything of importance? You'll wear the prescribed court dress. It's been *de rigueur* for hundreds of years. Our relatives will lend you the long train, the puffed sleeves. And from now on, Tant Hedvig will teach you how one curtsies at court," said mor happily. But the champagne cork that held down the bubbles of mockery popped out. Oh! I hooted with laughter.

Mor wept. "What will happen to you out in life? You laugh. Laugh. At everything. You take nothing that is serious—seriously. It is immensely important to be presented at court," mor said with passion.

A shiver went down my spine. I didn't feel frightened of what would happen to me in life. But suddenly I felt frightened of myself. It was true I laughed at everything. Was there something wrong with me? A burst of such wild merriment answered my question that I couldn't hold it back. "Oh, mor! Oh, mor!" I laughed.

———

Daily newspaper reading became part of my preparation for the new life that would be mine once I'd "come out." I would have to learn how to "converse," I was told. The sophisticated diplomats I'd meet were knowledgeable when it came to topics of the day. "Topics?" I asked my sister Greta. I was flicking through *Svenska Dagbladet,* the only newspaper my family would read, the sole news sheet that anyone of our circle as much as glanced at.

"It speaks only of sports. And of the doings of the royal family and of other 'important' Swedes," I said. I wondered if the factory women I met every day weren't "Swedes" too. Weren't their doings important? I told my thoughts to my sister.

"You're not to speak of your crèche once you've come out," Greta said. "You must never mention the ugly sides of life in elegant society."

"Ugly?" I thought. I was thinking of Gösta, who was lovelier than a rose!

Suddenly Greta pinched her nose. "Edit, you smell!" I told her I'd just returned from my crèche. "The children stink of shit. Of shit with worms in it," I said, and Greta backed away from me. But at that moment Tant Hedvig was announced by Hanna. And right away we began our curtsy lessons.

"You've acquired the knack," cried mor's stupid, kindly old friend who was going to present me at court. "Ah, child, I must find a husband for you quickly," beamed Tant Hedvig. "As soon as you've come out, I'll be looking about for a young man. It won't be difficult! I hear that you are popular with men. I also hear that you are a terrible flirt."

The goose smiled. Suddenly she stared in horror at my head. "What on earth! There is something moving about on your scalp. A louse!" Tant Hedvig shrieked. She jumped away from me—from the girl she was going to introduce to the world of royalty.

I laughed. Just the way Holger had taught me, I caught the louse and crushed it between my fingers, and pretended to be popping it into my mouth. "I've just come home from my crèche. The children's heads crawl with lice."

Tant Hedvig told Greta that her protégée must leave that repulsive world instantly. "Instantly!" she cried, dashing off to her round of lunches, teas, bridge games, supper parties. They filled her days to bursting point.

"You heard Tant Hedvig," Greta said. "You're not to return to your repulsive crèche, Edit. To your repulsive world!"

(Repulsive world?)

"Do you feel nervous?" Agnes asked me as ten of us lined up in the Hall of Mirrors, next to the Throne Room. "Sort of shivery?"

"Shivery?" I asked. "Why?"

"Well, scared you'll slip on the polished floors when we curtsy to the queen? Scared you'll make a fool of yourself?"

"I'll never make a fool of myself," I said. "People might think one a fool, but as long as one doesn't think so oneself, one isn't." But at that moment my friend's name was called.

"Fröken Agnes Weidenhielm!"

Count Mörner, nicknamed the "court-ape," straightened Agnes's yards-long train and motioned her forward toward the throne, where the monarch herself sat as stiff as a bread knife. Agnes curtsied. All the way to the floor. She managed beautifully. Then she moved on.

"Fröken Elsa Rosenblad!" the court ape cried, and dumpy Elsa stomped forward, curtsied awkwardly, all but toppled over.

When it came to my turn, I rehearsed what Tant Hedvig had told me: "Head up, eyes lowered, back as straight as your ancestors' swords. Remember to move softly. Like the court women of the olden days."

Fuck! I decided to walk as I always walked. Ignoring Tant Hedvig's commands, I stared straight into the eyes of Queen Viktoria. Good heavens! Was that creature Sweden's queen? Atop a skeleton-body, atop a scrawny neck, sat a sour lemon. And it was thanks to this obscure German princess that all upper-class Swedes were pro-German? Was it thanks to this foreigner that we Swedes had to go hungry, so the kaiser could feed his murder-armies?

"It wasn't very exciting, was it?" Agnes said as we returned to the Hall of Mirrors. Refreshments were waiting us.

"Death'll be jollier," I said. A feeling of despair

filled me. Oh, to get away from this palace! I thought. To leave the group of chatting girls. I hurried toward a tall window, where I hid behind the heavy curtains. I stood looking into the coal-black winter day, at the fierce snowstorm.

Oh, why did I suddenly feel so disconsolate? Lately weights of despair had been pressing me into the ground. I couldn't understand myself. Was one invaded by new feelings beyond one's control, I wondered? Without knowing why one felt melancholy? It was frightening.

I leaned my forehead against the cold window-pane and looked at the snow that was burying my city, beyond which ice-filled seas heaved and howled, burying the vast land of Russia.

Russia that kept experiencing upheavals, revolutions. What was re-vo-lu-tion? Mor turned pale at the word; her friends trembled when it was mentioned. True, the word sounded terrifying, as frightening as the snowstorm that smacked the cheeks of the Royal Palace, where I stood now hiding behind curtains of silk, the palace of Gustaf the Fifth and of his lemon-hued consort.

I felt I must get away. Get away! My mood of despair was strangling me.

"What's the matter with you?"

I didn't answer Agnes. For a second I stared at my childhood friend as if I'd never seen her before: something in my face made her step back. Agnes knew I was changing, that I was always in the process of changing. She used to say that I was unlike our friends.

She said: "Edit, we're off to the photographers. Come along! We're to be photographed in our court attire," she said excitedly.

I shook my head. "I haven't the money to pay a photographer!"

All at once I felt bitter. I'd never had a penny to buy anything for myself. I had always had to give my tiny birthday and Christmas gifts to settle gas bills and other wretched things. And now I couldn't go with my friends to have myself immortalized in my medieval court attire.

"I hate fancy costumes," I said. I pointed to my long train, the stiff, puffed sleeves, crisscrossed with black velvet ribbons. "A theatrical getup, lent me by relatives. I must give it back tonight. Well, I'm off."

Agnes let me go without a word, and I headed for one of the tall doors. In passing, I threw a look into the Throne Room. It was empty except for a withered lemon there on the throne—the color of mold.

I knew that I mustn't give way to fantasies. I felt that my fantasies were getting the better of me lately. "But are they fantasies?" I asked myself. Of course they are. Of course, no lemon, green, withered, moldy, is occupying the throne of Sweden.

———

"Sister! Gösta's mother's coming up the street. Running!" I flattened my nose against the window of the crèche. Although I no longer worked there, I paid it visits in order to—why, to see Gösta. I missed him! "Gösta's mother is coming to the crèche," I told sister excitedly.

"No, it's too early," she said. But peering through

the ice-flowers on the windowpane, she agreed with me. "It is the whore. What does she want?"

At that moment Gösta's mother burst into the crèche and hurled herself into sister's arms.

"I've killed him!"

"Him?"

"My fellow. I caught him with a tart. I kept giving him my earnings . . ."

I ran into the room where the children were playing, aimlessly hitting each other with dirty building blocks. I threw my arms about Gösta. I looked into his eyes—two tiny cups of hot tea. Till this moment I hadn't known I loved Gösta. Yes, I loved him!

And as I held him in my arms, I said wildly to life: "Give me a boy! Give me one day a little boy. Like Gösta! Give me," I commanded life, "give me!"

My emotional paroxysm was over as swiftly as it had come, and when Gösta's mother tore him from my embrace and scampered from the crèche with her son, I calmly asked of sister, "Is Gösta's mother really a murderess?"

"And a drunk! And a thief and a whore. The police will get her. The harlot will get her just deserts."

"And Gösta, sister? Will he get his just deserts?" I asked.

"*Madame la Comtesse, une tasse de thé?*"

Was my French correct? I wondered, as I and my friends served tea at the French embassy. More or less, I answered myself. The Frenchwoman had a bald patch on top of her head. *"Quel chevelure vous avez, mon enfant,"* she cackled enviously. "What hair!" I moved swiftly out of her acid, French aura. I hurried over to the American, Mrs. Johnson, who was laden with costume jewelry like a Christmas tree.

"Another bowl of tea? A—torte, Mrs. Johnson?" I asked the wife of the American attaché. Oh, my English was terrible. I should have said cup instead of bowl and pastry instead of torte. It was hard not to mix my four languages in the Babel of a diplomatic tea. I saw Agnes coping with the same difficulty across the glittering drawing room.

These endless teas! For six months I and the girls who had "come out" this year had had to attend balls, dinner parties, teas, receptions in order to learn the manners of *"le monde."* The boredom was so excruciating inside of me I howled like a dog. I could endure the silly ladies. But not their old husbands who, the minute they laid eyes on me and my fellow sufferers began to act like romping youngsters. The worst of the lecherous lot was the spiffed, American military attaché.

He sauntered up. Hypocritically he put his fat hand on his fat wife's arm, but it was me he gobbled up with his alcohol eyes.

"Our snow maiden!"

He knew that he had no chance with me and my fellow fledglings, but he put in a good word for his ambassador, or rather for his ambassador's son. "The lad has been boring himself silly during his holidays in your Nordic capital. The whole American colony will be relieved when Ambassador Morris's gloomy son returns to Harvard. The kid refuses to accept invitations to diplomatic functions. He rarely drinks, he never cracks a joke!

"You will come for dinner, Fröken Toll?" he said. "I know you're in great demand. You're always busy. Are you free Friday? Of course you've met the American ambassador—Ira Nelson Morris? Well, this is his son, young Ira. He is returning to the States. My wife and I are giving a little farewell dinner for him. Please accept! You'll come, won't you?" His thick fingers pinched my waist with the pitiful playfulness of a man of fifty. "Say yes," he giggled, already spiffed.

Another diplomatic dinner party? Another boring evening? I thought, and I grabbed a silver salver laden with pastry in the form of birds. I bore down on the English ambassador's wife. I pointed to the bevy of cakes that had descended on the salver on their clumsy wings of chocolate.

"A little chocolate bird, Lady Howard?" I asked the scraggy Englishwoman. There was a sound of despair in my voice, but I didn't know why. "A nice little chocolate bird?"

———

I groaned. I must have a respite. Remembering my disappearing trick at the Royal Palace, I hid myself behind the heavy window curtains. I wished the cackling diplomats were all dead. They'd stink less as corpses!

Suddenly I longed for my dead sister Elsa, whom I last saw in a metal container.

If Elsa was here, she'd look for me behind these curtains. She'd ask what ailed me. And I'd have to answer that I didn't know. I'd have to tell Elsa that I just went on and on, attending meaningless functions.

123

"What's the use?" I'd ask her. And I'd remember what she'd once told me. "If a child of three goes tricycling round and round and round, he'd be acting normally because of his age. If he did it when he was twenty, he'd be locked up in a lunatic asylum!"

"Perhaps you've been tricycling round too long by now, Edit."

"There is something wrong with me," I'd tell her.

She'd gaze at me with her eyes that saw through people. "Things do go wrong with one at times. Personally I think you've lost yourself. And there's nothing more dangerous. You must find the Edit you once were. The Edit you have lost is your child." Elsa would tell me, and I'd ask her if the child remained within one all one's life.

"Certainly," Elsa would say. And she'd smile. "I remember you at the age of four, Edit. In Sjögård. That Edit was the real you. That child was *you*."

"And that child went her own way," Elsa would say. "She never cared what anyone said. She played her own games. She'd take earwigs for rides although everyone made fun of her. And her favorite dancing partner was a goat. He'd pounce on his hind legs before her, and she'd hold his forelegs, and they'd hop about. And once I saw her take a hen's face in her hands and passionately kiss it. That Edit was on intimate terms with everything that lived."

"What else did she do?" I'd ask my sister.

"She gave away everything to children who had nothing. She made them a present of her mittens. And her wool bonnet. But when she gave away her knitted jacket, her Aunt Anna gave her a hiding. Edit spat in her face. She called her aunt names that I wouldn't care to repeat in this diplomats' drawing room."

"Fart-ass, I expect. Fart-idiot!" But suddenly I felt happy. I felt the way I'd felt when I was four, when I played with Holger and learned his vocabulary, and I stepped out from my hiding place and felt myself beaming on everyone.

———

Finally they caught me, shoved me into the Military Institute. "It will be hard on you, having to work," sighed mor. "I mean you being you."

It wasn't hard. I ignored my eight hours of screaming boredom, and galloped off to my real life the minute the clock struck five. I was always the first to leave, the last to arrive. I could have stood it if it hadn't been for my coworkers who kept discussing old age pensions when we munched our dry sandwiches at noon.

"At sixty we'll all of us receive old age pensions," they tittered ecstatically.

Sixty!

My getting to know the lives of office-slaves shook me more than my knowing peasant women in Sjögård and factory women in the crèche. They'd looked like lumps of filth bundled in rags. But the office workers looked like the sheets of dry paper on which they jotted down silly military sums forty hours a week.

"It's valuable experience for you to associate with serious women," my sister Greta said. "With women who think." She was jubilant because she'd got me into a cage as claustrophobic as her own office-hell.

"The trouble with you, Edit," she said, "is that you never think. Just gad about." I looked at her. Did a cow think? Then I looked into the pebbles that were Maud's stone-eyes. Did her pebbles think? Mor's eyes were ever bright with tears, but not with thoughts.

I began to observe people on my daily run between home and prison. Did those people on the streets think? The faces I saw looked like the asses of pigs with a tiny shithole for a mouth. When they jabbered away to their fellow pigs, only farts emerged.

Maybe one day I'd be like them. I'd start to "think" when it was time for me to receive my old age pension. When my mouth, like everyone else's, became a shriveled farthole, my gay dancing legs covered with varicose veins like those of my "colleagues" at the Military Institute. I laughed behind my face. I wouldn't be about at sixty to collect.

And meanwhile, each day at five I galloped off with my mane flying, off into a Stockholm the pension-hungry office girls didn't know, a Stockholm whose sun had a yellow, laughing belly, whose moon lolled luxuriantly in the sky that was its silken bed.

———

One day as I passed Grefturegatan and my old crèche, I felt like saying hello to sister. It was past closing time, but I knocked on the grimy door, waited, then knocked again. There was no answer, only a loud sob from inside the crèche. I gave the door a kick and it opened. It hadn't been locked.

"Sister!"

In the dark room a creature with its head in its arms lay sobbing against the grubby eating table.

"Gösta's set fire to himself, fröken! He burned like a torch!"

"Gösta? Burned?"

"Like a torch. The neighbors saw the police car drive off with his screaming mother, fröken. A moment later they saw a light in her deserted room in the garret. When they got there, Gösta had set fire to himself. They couldn't get near him. He choked to death. They found matches, kerosene . . ."

Sister and I were in each others' arms. She was no longer a bleating, pious sheep: she was a weeping working woman. She smelled like one of the many factory workers I'd met in the crèche. Now my nostrils picked up another familiar perfume. I remembered the odor of tears that permeated the shacks in which I'd played in Sjögård. The shacks of my childhood had stunk of tears. I sniffed. Yes. The smell that came from sister was the same smell that emanated from the wives of mormor's work-broken farmhands who had emigrated to America. Had tears, then, a perfume of their own, I wondered?

The scent of tears was the scent of my childhood, the scent of my playmates in faraway Sjögård.

I felt curiously at peace. Was the melancholia I tried not to recognize the result of my having lost the memory of the perfume of tears? Of having lost my childhood? Was the child one had been the most important part of one's being, the core from which emerged future emotions, future actions?

I trembled, and as I listened to the snowstorm that slapped against the dirty window of the crèche I asked myself in anguish: how did I lose Edit? How will I find her?

127

I sat near the American military attaché at his flower-adorned table. I didn't understand a word he said. My English was school English, taught by an Oxford-educated Swedish professor. But the American dialect spoken by the attaché sounded like weird grunts.

"You laugh at everything I say, Fröken Toll," he shouted in his booming voice. "I like that. Any man would. Why, you're the gayest young thing I've ever come across." He tossed down glass after glass of bubbling champagne.

He nodded in the direction of a boy I could see behind bowls of pink carnations. "That's young Morris," he said. "The glummest kid I've ever met."

I glanced at the foreigner who sat across the table staring into the lighted candles. I'd never seen such a sad face. It was thin, heart shaped. The wide brow was splendid. And what thoughtful eyes he had. He has a very lonely mouth, I thought.

"We're jolly glad he's off to Harvard," said the military attaché. "It's been heavy going trying to amuse someone who thinks the women of our diplomatic corps are either imbeciles or ladies of easy virtue. All he does is read. Emerson, that bore. The American colony in Stockholm will heave a sigh of relief when he returns to school."

"School? But he's a young man," I protested. The French secretary who sat on my other side guffawed. In his elegant French language, he explained that in backward America young men were referred to as "kids" and universities were dubbed "schools."

"An uncivilized nation, inhabited by illiterate immigrants," he said. His voice was full of scorn. "Young Morris is different. He is civilized. His father being a diplomat, he's had the luck to be educated in Europe. England, Switzerland, even Sweden. He didn't attend school in Stockholm, but he and his sister, and the two daughters of the British vicar, had classes with the sons of the crown prince, so that they'd get a chance to speak English. Ah, young Morris looks just like Rimbaud," the French secretary concluded, peering at the American through his monocle.

"He looks like Shelley," I said.

———

"Well, hello!"

The elderly crows had left "Shelley" and me alone in the middle of the brightly lit drawing room.

"Good night," I said.

Ira Morris corrected me almost angrily. "You mean 'good evening,' don't you? I'm going out of my mind with these dinners. You seemed to have a jolly time," he said grumpily. "You laughed at everything my father's attaché said. That drunken fool!"

"I laughed because I didn't understand his tongue. I understand your tongue better," I answered. I smiled into his big, sad eyes.

"It's so terrible here," he said.

"Terrible!"

"Let's get away. Let's get away from the ogres. The old witches," he said, but I answered that I didn't know what those words meant.

"I am not acquainted with the word *ogre*. I do not

understand *witch*," I laughed, and Ira's dark impatient eyebrows drew together.

"You jabbered away in French during dinner. You jabbered away in German before dinner. Why can't you speak proper English?" he asked sourly.

"I can quote Shakespeare if you wish," I said. "The first act of King Lear . . ."

"No, thank you!"

"I can also cite Molière. A little Schiller, too. Only Schiller is a bore."

"A bore! Schiller! The greatest of all German writers. A dedicated socialist."

I looked about me quickly. "The word *socialist* is taboo in Sweden," I murmured.

To my amazement, Ira threw his head back and burst into laughter.

"Taboo in the country of Branting? Branting, the father of new Sweden?"

Involuntarily I retreated a step. "You mustn't mention the name of that political agitator," I said, not daring to pronounce the name that my family and their circle abhorred.

What a strange boy this Ira Morris was. I wanted to get away from him. I didn't want to.

The American military attaché rolled up to us, purple from drink. "May one share the joke?" he asked. He looked at laughing Ira with amazement; but I gave the American boy a sign not to divulge the subject of our conversation. Branting and his associates must not be mentioned at an elegant, diplomatic party.

"I must now beg farewell of my hostess. Of your wife. I must return in haste to my mother's home," I added in my terrible English. "It might soon become midnight."

The American attaché hooted with alcoholic chortling. "Midnight, eh? Look, Cinderella! Let me take you home in my car." But I backed away from the fat, sweating man. Heavens! I didn't want to be alone with that pawing gorilla in a closed car.

"No. No, thank you," I said in panic. "I will catch hold of mine tram."

Once again the young American corrected my English.

"Catch a tram! Not 'catch hold' of a tram," he said grumpily, but I was already curtseying before my American hostess with her Christmas-tree jewelry. I turned round; I threw a last look at Ira. Our eyes met. And then my eyes met those of the American attaché, who waved to me. "Good night, snow maiden," he chuckled.

———

"A young foreigner asked for you while you were out," mor said. She sat huddled on her sofa.

"I didn't understand what he wanted. Nor why he came. He was dressed casually. He had casual manners. Oh, yes, now I remember," mor added in her vague way. "He left an invitation card to a ball at the residence of the American ambassador. The palace that used to belong to Prince Eugene! His parents are giving a ball for the crown prince of Italy whose ship has arrived in Stockholm's harbor."

Mor smiled to herself. "A charming youth. Much less stiff than our Swedish young men. Very gentle. He strolled about looking at what's left of Farmor Horn's antiques. He kept smiling to himself."

"Our last antiques were all sold this morning," said Greta, as she came marching into our minute sitting room. "Mor, we're penniless. Paupers. I've arranged for you to go and live with Moster Helga in Örebro. I'm taking a position in the country. It's a good thing that Maud's marrying. Edit has her job, thank God. Well, we'll be breaking up. High time. Our family's been held together too long with strings and safety pins."

Mor began to weep. But neither Greta nor I paid attention. She'd wept too often. Too long. "Where'll Edit go when you've shipped me off to Örebro?" she sobbed.

"I've seen to everything," said efficient Greta. "I've taken a room for her in the family boarding-house next door. Most suitable. It's run by the widow of an army captain. Edit will have a tiny room on the ground floor. But she'll be well looked after. I've asked the captain's widow to keep a strict eye on her."

"Where's my invitation card, mor?" I asked. I never listened to boring Greta. "Here it is!"

> The American Ambassador and Mrs. Ira Nelson Morris request the pleasure of the company of Fröken Edit Toll at the ball given in honor of His Royal Highness, Crown Prince Umberto of Italy, Friday the . . .

"That's tomorrow!" I shouted. "My balldress is in tatters. I've danced it to death. Yesterday I spilled something on it. Oh well, I'll pin a flower over the spot."

"It'll be your last ball," snapped Greta. "I'm told you're doing very bad work at the Military Institute. You sleep on the job, it seems. No wonder. You're out amusing yourself all the time. The captain's widow will see to it that you're in bed by ten. I've discussed your case with her."

"Case?" I laughed.

"Shit-ass," I called Greta behind my bland face. Was I to go to bed at ten, just when exciting Stockholm wakes up and reaches for me with a thousand arms? Greta had forgotten I had the longest, the swiftest legs in all of Stockholm, and that my room at the widow's was on the ground floor. When the beastly widow was snoring in bed, my legs would leap across the windowsill, I told myself. They'd carry me off to fun. Once again I snatched up my invitation card:

> The American Ambassador and Mrs. Ira
> Nelson Morris request the pleasure of the company of . . .

They will have the pleasure of my company, I said to myself. After all, didn't their son deliver the invitation himself, in order to make sure he'd have the pleasure of my company? Ira did! I liked his name. I liked him.

———

They reached my tits. The tiny Italian naval cadets flocked about us tall, Swedish girls, laughing with their white, Italian teeth. They made the Swedish girls laugh, too. I waltzed with them till I felt as wild as a bird at dawn.

"This is our dance, I believe," Ira told me sourly.

I thought him beautiful. Beautiful in a way that Swedes weren't beautiful. It was his expression. His dark eyes glowed; he had a poet's wistful mouth. It made me feel close to him. His lost, lonesome mouth spoke of some inner suffering. Was his melancholia related to mine? To my inside melancholia?

I laughed for joy at being in his arms.

"You laugh, you always laugh," Ira said as we danced. "At awful Hallet Johnson's awful dinner party, you didn't stop laughing. Tonight you laugh with the Italian midgets. Is it a tick?"

"Teek?"

"Tick! Do speak English. A tick is a spasm. Why do you laugh all the time?"

"I didn't know one laughed because of something. I laugh because I feel like laughing. Because I feel gay," I said.

It was so lovely to be waltzing with the American. I felt that I'd known him forever—since all eternity. He was as slender and willowy as myself, and I liked men to be supple and swift. I sighed in contentment. Ira looked down into my eyes as if his eyes were bees burrowing into the heart of a flower.

"We'll dance only with each other tonight," he told me. "Not with anyone else! Never with anyone else!

"By the way, my name is Ira," he said. And I said, "Mine's Edit."

"There's an Irish saint called Edita," Ira said. "She was sainted for her goodness of heart."

"But I'm no saint."

"So I hear," said Ira. "It seems you're a terrible flirt." He scowled. "You must stop that now that we've met."

"No, I'll only stop flirting when I'm dead, Ira."

"No, now!" he insisted.

"No, only in my coffin," I laughed. Ira laughed, too.

"You're laughing," I said. "It's the first time I've heard you laugh tonight. Why you laugh?" I asked in my terrible English.

"Well, you told me just now one didn't have to have a special reason to laugh. You said one only needed to feel happy. I feel happy. For the first time in my life. Happy Edit! Because we'll always be together. Always, Edit!"

We! "Always?" I said. A strange feeling gripped me. I've come home, I thought. I didn't know what I meant by I've come home, but I felt it. I settled deeply in Ira's embrace. He shivered, and I saw we were looking away from each other. We no longer danced close. From one minute to the next, things had become too serious between us, too serious for chatting, for laughing. We were oblivious of the music, of the boisterous Italian feet that bruised the floors.

The orchestra stopped, and Ira asked me to come upstairs with him. "We must talk, Edit. I have something urgent to ask of you. It concerns our future."

In a little upstairs room, the two of us sat stiffly facing one another on two stools, upholstered in satin. We still kept our eyes averted, still didn't speak. Ira was pale, almost white. He repeated he wanted to discuss our future.

"Edit, I want to become a writer. Do you mind? My father wants me to become a diplomat, like himself. I refuse. If you have nothing against it, Edit, I'd like to become a writer."

"I am one."

"Not a writer, Edit?"

"A small writer. Last week I solded a story to *Vec-*

kojournalen. It means *Weekly Journal* in Swedish. I got paid fifty crowns. I buyed these little silk slippers."

"They are decorated with blue tassels," Ira said.

"Yes, little blue tassels. They are my first pretty dance slippers. I love them so very much," I said, and Ira's eyes filled with tears.

"I love *you* so terribly much," he whispered. "I love your little slippers terribly much, too!" Suddenly he knelt before me, kissing the blue tassels on my dance slippers.

"Edit, I have been lonely all my life. Now, suddenly, I'm not lonely."

"I'm so lonely, too!"

"You? You're surrounded by people. You're popular in Stockholm," Ira said. "I've seen it with my own eyes."

"I'm lonely within me," I said. "Inside my own self."

"Oh, Edit."

"Ira," I whispered, and we looked into each other's eyes. We were amazed at what had happened to us.

A fat woman wearing ropes of pearls stomped into the room. Her frog eyes bulged.

"What are you two up to," she said. "I'd like to know. All alone up here?"

Ira leapt to his feet.

"Mother! Edit—Edit Toll is a writer. Like me! She has already sold a story. *Sold* one!" he said. Although his face blazed with newfound happiness, his fat mother noticed nothing. She ogled me with jealous eyes, and I felt it was at that moment—at that very second—she lost her son.

"I insist on knowing what you've been up to here—all alone," she said again, but Ira paid no attention to her. He grabbed my hand and I knew he had parted with his childhood and would never return to it. He led me downstairs, where crowds of young people were dancing cheek to cheek, and where the orchestra played happily "You and Me Make We." I felt that Ira wanted to put as great a distance as possible between me and his mother.

"You and Me," played the orchestra, and Crown Prince Umberto of Italy came out on the shining floor with Ira's sister Constance in his arms. How sad Ira's beautiful sister looked, I thought, as we followed the couple onto the dance floor. Is it because of the ogress upstairs? I wondered. Ira, too, gazed at his pale sister. His body trembled. I pressed my cheek to his.

"Don't think of her," I whispered. "She's dead."

"Dead?"

"Everyone who is wicked is dead," I answered.

"Do you know that for a fact?" asked Ira, and I nodded.

"My parents are both ogres," Ira said. "Rich people like them corrupt everyone they come into contact with. They've ruined my sister. They shan't ruin me. They won't as long as you're about. You will be about, won't you, Edit?" Ira said. He buried his face in my hair. "You will, won't you?"

"Be about, Ira?"

"Yes. About, about. *About!*"

———

But in the taxi we had no time to talk. With Ira's mouth glued to mine, I couldn't breathe, much less speak. Oh! The two of us might suffocate, I thought, we might die if we didn't let go of each other's lips. At long last we got to my door. We stood on the snowy pavement. We looked at each other. We were stupefied by what had happened to us.

"We'll marry before I return to Harvard. We'll marry right away, Edit!" Ira said.

"But I may have to marry Staffan," I said.

"You . . . you mean you are engaged?"

"Since one little week. Before I meeted you, Ira," I said.

Ira was as pale as the snow that was building a roof on his fur cap. "I've never been happy before tonight," he said. "Never. Tonight I felt my awful loneliness was over. For good! Now there's nothing left to me to do except to kill myself."

"Oh, Ira, no! I'll be engaged to you, too. To Staffan and you."

"But you can't be engaged to two men, Edit!"

"I was almost engaged to three men once!"

"But you can't marry more than one."

"Perhaps I will marry no one. I'm too little. I mean, I'm too young to marry."

Ira grabbed my shoulders and shook me so hard that snowflakes flew from my hair like white bees.

"You can't live with more than one man at a time, Edit. You can't belong to two—males." He gave me a long look.

"You do know what it means to belong to a man, don't you, Edit? You know what marriage means?"

"What means it, marriage?"

Ira groaned. I sneezed.

"I've catched a catch-cold!" I said.

"A cold! I've caught a cold!" Ira corrected me angrily. I leaped into the doorway of the house. "I've catched a catch-cold, Ira!" I laughed and sneezed again. I kissed the frozen insides of my hands and I scattered my kisses in the direction of my love. I pushed open the front door. I felt so happy. "Oh, Ira!"

He stood looking after me. Didn't his mouth already look less lonesome? Yes, Ira's mouth looked as if he'd never be lonesome again.

———

"So where did you dance all night? Whom did you flirt with?" Ira asked me in the small boat that flung us about on the heaving bay of Stockholm.

"I danced all night at the Minister of State. He used to be a labor agitator. He is called Hjalmar Branting."

"*Called* Hjalmar Branting!"

Ira sounded so furious with me that I looked at him, astonished. But our little boat soared, sat atop a wave, slid into a trough of water, and I looked away from him. I liked big, bad waves.

"Branting didn't know how to receive properly," I said. "He and his poor wife looked awkward. Ill at ease. Bothered. You see, they come from a different' class than mine," I added. I was so fascinated with the boat's antics that I didn't notice the change on Ira's face. It had turned to stone.

"What's wrong, Ira?" I asked. I felt worried.

"Class!" He snorted. "Never use that filthy word again. I told you that Branting is a giant Swede. Was, rather! Now he's old fashioned. Newer, bolder men have moved to the front. But Branting and his fellows started it all! They created a new Sweden!"

"New Sweden?" I said.

Ira, steering our small boat, didn't look up at me, and I stood gazing toward the quai where the Royal Palace stood, as heavy and bad-tempered as always. I peered through the snow at the House of Nobles, where my family's shield hung and where my kin held dinners with the king's footmen serving at table.

But our pitching craft was taking in water: I began to bail it out.

"A foreigner has to teach you about your own country," Ira still sounded angry. "Edit, the Sweden of your early childhood was a pigsty. Half of your country fled to my country. To America! But men like Branting transformed Sweden into a home for Swedes. Tailor Palm, Danielson, all of Branting's friends went to jail for their faith. So do Sweden's new men! Some are in prison at this moment."

I continued to bail.

"They are religious, you mean?" I asked. "Is that what you are saying?" I asked Ira above the storm.

"Yes!" he shouted. "Their religion is world socialism. Sweden's new men believe that Sweden's soil and Sweden's mines and Sweden's forests belong to Swedes. To all Swedes! They believe in equal distribution of your country's great riches. They believe in the rights of men!"

Ira banged his fist angrily against the side of our heaving boat.

"Edit, you're an ignoramous! You're as ignorant as a poor servant girl who's been deprived of education. I suppose you've never heard of our American giants either. The real Americans. Not dressed-up monkeys like my father, nor apes like his military attaché. Nor toy soldiers like the men of your family. Shame on you, Edit, for being so ignorant. One can't speak to you. You know nothing. Nothing!"

He was in a raging temper. When he looked up at me and saw I was weeping, he seemed astonished. He'd thought of me as a sort of "Viking." As someone who was strong, who always laughed. Now he saw the Viking crying. A girl he didn't know. A girl who was so ashamed of herself that she'd like to throw herself into the sea.

He reached out and took my wet hand. He drew me into the crook of his arm. He explained to me, gently, that my ignorance about the only thing that mattered—human beings—had upset him.

"Was I rough with you?" he said contritely. "Edit, you were put into a straitjacket at birth," he explained. "The moment you were born they tied you up in a straitjacket. By they, I mean your outmoded family. By they, I mean the ignorant teachers in your snob school, your church that tried to pervert you with their obsolete superstitions. Your entire social circle! Your whole bloody class!"

"What is it, a straitjacket, Ira?"

"Edit, they put dangerous madmen into straitjackets! And no creature is as dangerous as a newborn baby. Such as we all were once. Such as I was, such as you were. A new, wild baby is mad to live, mad to do new, unexpected, useful things, such as remaking our world. Quick! Let's put the dangerous little creature into a straitjacket. Edit, the ruling classes, the have-classes in all countries clamp their offspring into the straitjackets of conformity the moment they're born. Into the straitjacket of ignorance of the true aim of life. I, too, have been straitjacketed. But I'm breaking out. Shall I help you to break out too, Edit? Shall I, my darling? Darling, you're weeping."

I smelled the salt water, the salt tears on my lips. I kept on crying in the crook of Ira's arm.

"You weep like a little child," he whispered. "Like a terribly small child. I was rough with you," he murmured. "I've no manners when I'm upset. You see, my paternal grandfather was a butcher."

"Butcher? Mine, too. All my father's ancestors were butchers," I said.

"Yours? Butchers?"

"Yes, they slaughtered young men instead of young pigs! Sweden's kings knighted them because of that. I have the title 'honorable' because my ancestors were so very good at slaughtering." I sprang to my feet. And as I stood there in the heaving boat with my hair whirling about me, I shouted to Ira: "Turn back. I want to go home. I want to . . . to . . ."

"To what?"

"To think," I said. "I've never really known what it is to think!"

I felt happy. Something in me, long sickening, had suddenly been healed.

Ira seemed to hold his breath as he looked at me. I felt he was thinking, Will the poor prisoner succeed in freeing herself? Will she be able to wriggle out of the straitjacket she's been choked in since the moment she sprang into life? I will help her! I'll free my suffering girl.

Perhaps he didn't think all this, but I felt he did! He gazed at me with soft, tender eyes. He looked so young. Well, I was terribly young, too. The knowledge that we were both young made me happy. Oh, I said to myself, Ira and I belong to the youth of the world. Youth means victory, victory for everyone! Youth means life! I felt happy. To live—it is lovely, I thought to myself.

———

The day Ira's third book parcel arrived, I broke with mor for good. She looked up at me from her place by the fire and told me to throw the American's firebrand literature into the trash can. I refused violently. I belonged to the American now. To Ira! No longer to mor! Ira had told me that he wanted an adult wife, a wife who could share his thoughts, his feelings, his actions. He said he wanted a life companion who'd read every book that had been written by men who were changing the world, men who thought new, who felt new, who acted new.

"I shall devour every book that feeds my starved brain, mor," I said. "They're important books. They talk about important subjects. I've never read anything like them before. Not once in my whole life. I didn't know such books existed. Now I do know."

But mor groaned. "I pity the mother of that horrid young rebel," she sighed. "The mother of young Morris. She must be tearing her hair out in tufts."

"Don't worry about her," I said. "Her diamond tiaras will hide the bald spots." I told mor it was Ira's paternal grandfather who had earned the fortune which his mother now squandered on jewels, furs, luxury cars.

"He pumped the blood from his laborers' veins. He worked his immigrant slaves to death in his freezing slaughterhouse in Chicago, Ira told me. He's going to write about it. He says that our slave drivers do the same as America's slave drivers. The wives of Sweden's rich men also wear jewels and furs, Ira says."

"Ira says! Ira says! Please don't parrot your Chicago gangster. Edit, I forbid you to see him again," cried mor.

But with Ira's help I'd divested myself of my straitjacket. I looked at mor with pity. Ought I to tell her that I and Ira were already married? Oh, how beautiful our marriage ceremony had been! In the snow-covered Lilyans Woods. It had lasted three minutes. We had remained on our skis throughout the ceremony, and my husband-to-be had pronounced our marriage vows.

"Edit, repeat my words after me," he'd said. "My words are more binding than those we'll say later at a registrar's office. I'll pronounce them slowly so that you'll get your English right."

"Edit, you are my forever one and only!" he'd said, and I felt as grave as my husband did, when I repeated the vow.

"Ira, you are my forever one and only," I whispered. We'd become man and wife. We skied away from the silent woods. We knew we were wedded for all eternity.

But now, in front of the fire, mor wept her never-ending tears.

"Oh, don't weep, mor!" At long last I felt exasperated, but I spoke gently. "At times you wept tears of pity, mor! For you are capable of pity! Ira says that very few people are. I intend to do something with the lake of tears I carry inside me. Ira says active tears transform themselves into revolt. A revolt that will change our world, mor. Isn't it beautiful?" I cried.

But locked in her confining straitjacket, she understood nothing. Suddenly she began to look like an old woman—which she wasn't. She shook her head; she muttered something incoherent. I felt that mor had died within her straitjacket. Poor little mor! I bent down. With passionate pity, I kissed her nose.

"Your nose, mor, your little nose." I felt such a tremendous love for her.

"Telephone, Edit!"

Greta was helping the packer to nail the crates he'd take to storage that evening, and as I went through the hallway, I glanced into the last crate to be nailed down. It was full of my schoolbooks—full of my dreadful misinformation. And my toys! I looked at my old toy soldiers, suitable playthings for a descendant of generals and marshals of Sweden, I thought, and I watched the packer lift his hammer to drive a huge nail into the crate that was the coffin of my musty, ignorant schoolbooks, of my lethal toys.

———

"It's me, Edit. I'm leaving for the station," said Ira over the phone. "Edit, do come to the station. I'm ill for you. I must see your face. If I don't, I shall die! Edit, are you there?" he asked in anguish.

I was there! But I didn't trust my voice. I choked down a sob. "Ira, I've told you I won't come to the station," I said. "If I did, I'd jump on your train."

"I beg you. We'll be married aboard ship. To-night!"

But I'd become adult. Divested of my straitjacket. I felt free, strong, decisive. I felt—*Edit*.

"We've discussed it. You must work! You must prepare yourself for us! I'll marry you the moment you return. I've promised you. Ira, I can't speak any longer." I was crying.

"I'm going to jump into a taxi. I'll be at your house in ten minutes," Ira said. I heard a strange sound. A sob? "Edit, show yourself to me in your bedroom window! At least let me see your face once more. You will, won't you? Say you will!"

I'd hung up. I didn't want Ira to hear me crying; he would remain in Stockholm. Did all couples who loved weep like me and Ira? Or was it that we were so terribly in love? So terribly young?

I went into my bedroom, from where the furniture had been removed as in the rest of the flat. The only things that were left were my bed and the white tulle curtains at the windows. I heard Ira's taxi drive up, but I didn't part the transparent curtains. I didn't dare to. I saw his face turned upward in the falling snow, but I didn't move. By now I knew my Ira! I knew myself! If we looked into each other's eyes once more, we'd be lost. Once locked in one another's arms, we'd never separate.

How beautiful my husband is, I thought, looking at his wistful, pining face. Something had happened to his lonesome mouth. It was lonesome no longer. Was that my doing? Had we already begun helping each other to live? He had ripped off my straitjacket; I'd taken away his lonesomeness. How marvelously he resembled young Shelley, I thought worshipfully. No, he was more like Alyosha in *The Brothers Karamazof*. All goodness. I was wrong again! He was Ira. Just Ira.

At that moment of overwhelming love, I forgot all caution and showed myself in the window. I drew back quickly. If Ira saw me, he wouldn't have the strength to remain a year in the faraway land where he must prepare himself for our joint life. Would ours be a turbulent life? It would be a life full of meaning. No straitjacket existence for us.

I put my hand into the opening of the tulle curtains and waved.

Ira's face lit up with the same joy and longing I felt for him. I saw his lips move, and I knew what he was saying. In the silence, I repeated our marriage vows.

"Ira, you are my forever one and only," I whispered. "My one and only!"

———

The taxi drove off with a grinding sound. Then I heard another sound, a loud "Bang!" It came from the hallway. The packer must be banging his last nail into the crate that contained my childhood. Yes, that was just what he was doing. I ran into the little hall, and I saw him drive a last huge nail into my childhood-crate. My eyes filled with tears. It surprised me. Then, just as surprisingly, I heard myself laugh.

"Bang!" I laughed. "Bang!"

Stockholm–Paris–New York